Sources of Civilization in the West

Crane Brinton and Robert Lee Wolff,
General Editors

Frank E. Manuel, the editor of this volume, received his A.B., A.M., and Ph.D. from Harvard University, where he has also taught in the Department of History, Government, and Economics. He is now Professor of History and Psychology at Brandeis University. He has lived in France and elsewhere on the Continent, and studied at the École des Hautes Études Politiques et Sociales in Paris on a Rogers Traveling Fellowship. Professor Manuel was a Guggenheim Fellow, 1957-1958, and has recently been made a Fellow of the American Academy of Arts and Sciences. He is the author of *The Age of Reason, The Eighteenth Century Confronts the Gods, Isaac Newton, Historian,* and *Shapes of Philosophical History,* in addition to numerous articles on eighteenth- and nineteenth-century social and intellectual history.

ALREADY PUBLISHED

The Crisis of Church & State, 1050-1300, *by Brian Tierney (with selected documents)*, S-102
The English Reform Tradition, 1790-1910, *edited by Sydney W. Jackman,* S-120
The Enlightenment, *edited by Frank E. Manuel,* S-121

FORTHCOMING VOLUMES

The Ancient World, *edited by Zeph Stewart*
The Renaissance, *edited by Werner Gundersheimer*
The Protestant Reformation, *edited by Lewis Spitz*
The Catholic Reformation, *edited by Theodore K. Rabb*
The French Revolution, *edited by Philip Dawson*
Nineteenth-Century Intellectual History, *edited by Richard L. Schoenwald*

THE

 # ENLIGHTENMENT

Edited by

Frank E. Manuel

 PRENTICE-HALL, INC.

A SPECTRUM BOOK *Englewood Cliffs, New Jersey*

Current printing (last digit):

11   10   9   8   7   6   5   4   3

FOREWORD

Historians are greatly addicted to finding turning points in history: events, processes, periods which mark a striking change in the way things are. Ever since the familiar Ancient, Medieval, Modern sequence for Western or European history was set up some four or five centuries ago, historians have sought to pin point the beginning of the modern. The favorite choices have commonly been such dates as the invention of printing (c. 1450), the discovery of America (1492), the Lutheran revolt (1517). More broadly, the "Renaissance and Reformation," considered as spread out over the fifteenth and sixteenth centuries, were accepted as marking the end of the medieval world, and the beginnings of our modern world. It can, however, be argued that—important as were all the complex changes, material as well as spiritual, symbolized by "Renaissance and Reformation"—the critical change, the "take-off point" for our modern democratic society, was rather the seventeenth and eighteenth centuries, the Enlightenment or Age of Reason, the subject of Professor Manuel's collection of documents.

For, though the beginnings, the rumblings, of democracy and the democratic focus on this world, on the "pursuit of happiness" for all, on the unhampered freedom of the scientist to investigate, of the engineer and entrepreneur to build, can be traced back even into the Middle Ages, it was not until a great many men and women thought and felt in ways represented by the documents in this book that our own struggling, tense, energetic, still at bottom hopeful society really came into being. These writers are essentially our Founding Fathers even, perhaps above all, in the United States. Professor Manuel here wisely lets them speak for themselves, with no more than the necessary introductory remarks. They are a remarkable group, inevitably in that dawn more hopeful, more full of the joy of life, than we can readily be. But they were by no means "terrible simplifiers." To study them now ought to be for us a salutary experience, a chastened renewal of hopes so badly—so naturally—diminished in this age of wars, hot and cold, of memories of depression, of existentialist whistling in the dark. For the Enlightenment did once enlighten, and may still do so.

Crane Brinton
Professor of History
Harvard University

CONTENTS

III. HUMAN NATURE

IV. LIBERTY & JUSTICE

V. THE FUTURE PROSPECT

Introduction

In the Middle Ages intellectual life rested securely in the hands of a priestly class. The spiritual revolution of the Protestant Reformation was still dominated by religious leaders who belonged to an ecclesiastical establishment. Only in the course of the seventeenth and eighteenth centuries did an independent secular class of popular philosophers gain prominence. Perhaps the Renaissance humanists had served them as forerunners and prototypes. One thing is certain: with the appearance of this new group of intellectuals the cleavage was sharpened within Western European society between the official bodies of priests and ministers of all religions and a loose assemblage of lay thinkers intent upon usurping many of their functions.

Who were these newcomers that were outside the pale of the churches? They were as varied and heterogeneous as intellectuals are today: doctors like John Locke; university professors like Adam Smith, Cesare Beccaria, and Immanuel Kant; versatile men-of-letters like Voltaire, Hume, Wieland, and Lessing; aristocratic judicial and administrative officials like Montesquieu, Turgot, and Condorcet; priests harboring secret heresy like Jean Meslier or abbés like Galiani who were simply heedless of religion. Perhaps most important of all were the free-lance writers—the Diderots and the Rousseaus, who began their careers as bohemians eking out an existence in Grub Street. A few managed to earn a tolerable living by writing alone, without recourse to a Maecenas, or to another job. One of them, Voltaire, wielded his pen so skillfully that he amassed a sizable fortune.

Sometimes working in isolation and sometimes organized in powerful cliques, the eighteenth-century intellectuals raised the curtain on a new world. They took a fresh and brazen look at reality. Nothing like it had occurred since the Greeks of the fifth

1

century before Christ. They ranged over the whole field of knowledge which had once been the province of the Church, and presented a different view of the physical world, of the nature of man, of society, of religion, and of history.

While there were great philosophic systematizers among them, for the most part they were popularizers. Addison prided himself on having brought philosophy out of the closet and into the coffeehouse. In France they were called *philosophes* rather indiscriminately, and they availed themselves of every known literary medium to teach their heterodox doctrines. Though these intellectuals quarreled with one another, and often acrimoniously, over theoretical details, they nevertheless expressed a common temper. They had a sense of the grandeur and the unprecedented nature of their enterprise: they were deliberately effecting a revolution in the fundamental beliefs of mankind. Despite national idiosyncrasies, their movement was cosmopolitan. Its protagonists were joined in a conviction that the past, particularly the Middle Ages, had been dark and that they were of the new dawn—the age of enlightenment, of *illuminismo*, of *Aufklärung*, the *siècle des lumières*, as it was called in their various languages.

England was the major source of novelty in thought, France the great continental transmitter. King Voltaire's wit was the keenest weapon. The *Encyclopédie*, which began to be published in 1751 under the direction of Diderot and d'Alembert, was the new *summa* of knowledge meant to rival and replace that of the medieval schoolmen. Though the movement was primarily Western European, its influence immediately extended to the American colonies, and outstanding figures of the Revolution—above all Jefferson—were steeped in the writings of the *philosophes*.

But before discussing the credo of these intellectuals of the Enlightenment, one should briefly recall the religious and political atmosphere in which they operated. Official state religions were everywhere installed and exacted a high price for apostasy. In Catholic France Protestants had no legal status after the Revocation of the Edict of Nantes in 1685. Episcopal England did not always make it easy for either Catholics or Dissenters to live unmolested. In Lisbon a victim was burned in an auto-da-fé as late as 1739. Acts of sacrilege were punishable by death in France and sorcerers were still burned as criminals in Austria. The Inquisition claimed its victims in Italy.

Everywhere petty crimes were cruelly punished. Local magistrates could be capricious and corrupt. Outside of England individuals had few secure rights unless they were members of the privileged classes, and even in England the renowned habeas corpus was more often a theoretical than a practical protection for those caught in the toils of the law.

When the *philosophes* ventured to raise the fundamental issues of man and society, they were treading on far more dangerous ground than the physical scientists of the previous age. By the end of the seventeenth century a truce had been established between science and religion. True, the burning of Giordano Bruno at the stake in Rome in 1600 was still remembered and Galileo had recanted his Copernican views as recently as 1633; but generally, even on the continent, scientific experiments were no longer considered subversive. Physical scientists either rendered lip-service to religion or they established a sharp line of demarcation between the provinces of religion and of physical science. Of course some great scientists, like Pascal and Newton, were devout believers.

In contrast to the scientists, writers on social, moral, and psychological subjects during the Enlightenment were engaged in hazardous occupations. They raised questions about man and his soul, not inanimate nature; about the origins and character of religion; about the sanctions of the social order; about the sources of state authority. Inevitably their impertinent curiosity struck at the foundations of organized religion and organized government.

The typical eighteenth-century literate citizen of the world believed that Newton's laws of motion and his world-system were a perfect model of science—even if he could not remotely follow the mathematical proofs of the *Principia*—and that the model was directly applicable to the "science of man" as well as to physical science. At the same time he revered Francis Bacon's inductive experimental method as the only true path to knowledge. He also accepted Descartes' conception of reason as clear and distinct ideas founded on methodical doubt of intellectual authority inherited from the past, especially that of Aristotle and of the scholastic philosophers. Above all, this "average intellectual" of the Enlightenment was enchanted by John Locke's *Essay Concerning Human Understanding,* with its sensationalist psychology that denied the existence of innate ideas and demonstrated how all complex reflections had their origins in simple impressions written on the "clean slate" of the mind.

The philosophical positions bequeathed by the luminaries of the seventeenth century were not always technically consistent one with another. But the ordinary person was able to assimilate the ideas of all four of these precursors of the Enlightenment without being troubled by their contradictions. Together this quadrumvirate provided the massive pillars for the erection of a towering new philosophical edifice that began to crowd out the traditional medieval Catholic as well as the Protestant world-view.

Like every total system the eighteenth-century structure had to meet certain basic intellectual needs: one, a plausible account—a replacement of Genesis—of the past of mankind; two, a theory and a tactic of social reform—the *philosophes* thus arrogated to themselves the functions of a Church militant; and three, a vision of the future of mankind on earth, instead of in heaven. The eighteenth century did in fact evoke an image of the past, propose an action program for the present, and dream a utopia of future bliss.

The battle over the past raged around the idea of original sin. Crucial for the traditional theology of all Christian sects, whether Protestant or Roman Catholic, had been the belief that man after the Fall was naturally corrupt, and that from the time of Adam this corruption had been passed on through every successive generation. Religious Christians might disagree about the precise ritual that could lead to salvation, but not about the initial disastrous event in Eden and its consequences. This doctrine explained the existence of evil in the world and it justified suffering. Original sin, moreover, helped to sustain theories of absolute obedience to the state. Since the natural evil in man had to be curbed, to be repressed by some external force established by God, kingship by divine right was eminently acceptable. In traditional Christianity the soul of man is a stormy field of battle between good and evil. A sense of the violence of this conflict in the bosom of every man had been accentuated rather than weakened by Protestant theology. Reformation divines could not really do anything about the man who had succumbed to the wiles of the devil (of whose real existence they were all profoundly convinced) except abandon the sinner to fire and brimstone in the hereafter. Protestant exaltation of the omnipotence of God had been accompanied by a denigration of ordinary human capacities and their significance.

In combatting the idea of original sin, eighteenth-century thinkers seem to have picked up many Renaissance humanist threads. The intellectual development of modern Europe does not necessarily move in a simple, unilinear direction. One way of examining the Enlightenment is to think of it as a resumption of the Renaissance, jumping over the world of the Reformation and Counter-Reformation with its rather dark and pessimistic picture of human frailty. Instead of the belief that by nature man was evil, Voltaire and Rousseau, Hume, Morelly, and Helvétius all held the conviction that man was by nature good, or at least neutral. If he was naturally good then the good in him should be allowed to express itself; if he was neutral then he could easily be persuaded to the good by education. There was no innate viciousness to overcome. The Renaissance idea of the free play of spirit was reasserted. This does not mean that the majority of literate people in the eighteenth century ceased to give obeisance, formal or real, to the dogmas of the church, or that they shunned its portals. Most men continued to observe the sacramental practices established in their respective countries. But what counts is the new spirit of the age. Despite overt religious conformity and even nominal acceptance of the doctrine of original sin, many came to regard man as by nature good, or at least capable of becoming good. Given a proper environment he would be gentle, loving, and unwarlike. He had a natural benevolence and a natural sympathy for other men. If he was not yet ruled by reason, he was on the way to that summit. To be sure, one school of thought insisted that human beings operated only out of self-interest. But even those who held to this opinion maintained that if men were allowed to function freely without the intrusion of alien political and religious influences, the natural harmony of selfish interests would create an ideally good society.

That man in a state of nature was good is one of those seductive myths which seems eternally recurrent. It had roots in antiquity, but the eighteenth-century writers revived it with a vigor and expounded it with a cogent forcefulness that had not been known before. The essential man deep-down, the real man, is good.

Fortified by this great myth of natural goodness, the age of Enlightenment came to express a buoyant optimism. A feeling of power over nature, both physical and human, did not derive from the myth alone. Many material factors also bolstered the spirit of confidence. It was strengthened by the new technology, the accumulation of wealth, the discovery and colonization of lands throughout the world, the organizational achievements of the dynastic states, the "relative peace" brought by the European balance of power, the relaxation of old social boundaries, and the emergence of a middle class. But whatever the contributing factors, natural man was the symbol leading the age out of medieval darkness.

And yet, if an eighteenth-century man looked about him, was there not also a flagrant discrepancy between this naturally good man and his conduct? What about evil in the world? When the philosophers went into the streets of Paris and London, when they followed men into the salons and watched them in a multiplicity of human relationships, what did these keen psychological observers see? Fops and dandies at Louis XV's court. Malice, envy, avarice, intrigue, treachery, violence rampant everywhere. Literature showed them that destructive warrior heroes were eulogized. Religious history taught them that men had tortured their fellows in the chambers of the Inquisition and had massacred them in century-long wars over minutiae of dogma. How could the eighteenth-century philosopher conciliate the ideal of natural man with his palpable experience of a wicked, vicious, oppressive creature?

One reply was that the man in the street was not a natural man, but an artificial one. How did he get that way? Surely not as a consequence of any inborn corruption or original sin. During the course of history evils had been generated externally, by society, the environment. They were the ugly encrustations of time. Thus the problem of man, which had once been understood as religious, became social. We witness the birth of "social science"—the term itself was introduced toward the end of the eighteenth century. Man was a victim of bad social conditions.

Some theorists like Rousseau went so far as to condemn all the arts and sciences perfected through the ages, all the uses of civilization, as destructive of the natural goodness and virtue of man in the state of nature. Most eighteenth-century writers, however, were not absolutist in this manner, and instead of denouncing society they concerned themselves with reforming it. If the world environment was unfavorable, there was an obligation to change it and thereby restore the natural goodness of human kind. Transforming social institutions, these meliorists obstinately contended, would alter and improve the behavior of their fellow men.

Here we stand at a great divide. Orthodox Christians were committed to the belief that "illumination" must first occur within man, that he must change his own soul after a spiritual struggle with evil. Religious thinkers of the seventeenth century such as Pascal were contemptuous of busy outward activities, which they interpreted as mere distraction from the metaphysical problems of existence. In opposition, a common eighteenth-century view was that evil resides not in man but in what bad custom and false belief, inherited from the past, had imposed on him. These are still basic alternative ways of looking at human nature and each has its partisans to this day: there are thinkers who place primary emphasis on individual internal transformation and those who would first attack the prevailing social system to bring about a renovation of man. Many, of course, take the compromise position that man is a product both of his nature and his environment, that religious conversion and social reform are not mutually exclusive.

In either event a number of questions pressed themselves upon the Enlightenment's upholders of natural goodness. What was this evil that had made men vicious and miserable? A somewhat tautological answer ran: evil is what natural man is not. If natural man is moved by the pleasure-pain principle, if he tests worth by utility, if he believes in the possibilities of terrestrial happiness, anyone who subscribes to divergent concepts has by definition succumbed to evil. With natural utility and the pleasure-pain principle as the foundation of his code of ethics, the eighteenth-century moralist could summon every one of the historical institutions of state and society, of religion and church before the bar of philosophical judgment. Have these institutions actually fulfilled the needs of man? If not, then they should either be reformed or destroyed.

The specific historical origin of evil was somewhat more perplexing. How had reasonable, naturally virtuous human beings ever fallen so far from nature that they had lapsed into the habit of disregarding the pleasure-pain and utility principles, and had abandoned altogether the quest for earthly happiness? In general, there were two ways of explaining the inception of evil in the history of man. One view likened the man who had violated the simple principles of natural behavior to a person stricken with a physical ailment. Or again, man was depicted as having drifted into error through weakness; he had misinterpreted nature because of faulty reasoning on first impressions. Unfortunately the piling up of errors and misconceptions through the ages had brought about the most severe of all illnesses, human unhappiness. And the cure for this malady was man's restoration to psychic good health through a renewed belief in the sound principles of philosophy, natural and moral. The *philosophes* whose writings are represented in this volume conceived of themselves as doctors ministering to the sick souls of humanity.

There was another view of the origin of evil that was perhaps more revolutionary in its political consequences. This theory ascribed the beginning of wickedness in the world to a historic plot of one group of men against their fellows. Sometime in the dim past—they were rather vague about the date—mankind had been poisoned by priests and tyrants whose lust for power was "unnatural." These persons were the monsters of the human order, the equivalent of abnormalities in the animal world. Such a radical intellectual position menaced existing institutions far more than the medical analogy of evil as ill health or debility. If you supposed that at an unknown historical moment priests and tyrants had conspired together to impose their will upon other men and that in order to maintain their domination they had forced evil, erroneous, and unnatural superstitions upon all mankind, then an inevitable corollary was the duty to liberate men by deposing the existing rulers of society, who were the direct descendants of the primeval plotters and usurpers of power.

Most *philosophes,* however, were not active political revolutionists. Their fear of anarchy was greater than their abhorrence of tyranny, and they would not have welcomed the rising of the masses, whom they regarded as the most benighted elements in the population, the very heart of darkness. Many of the reformers thought that they could convert the rulers themselves to philosophy, transform them into philosopher-kings, and inaugurate the age of enlightenment. The monarchs should be very strong in order that they might be very good—only thus could they succeed in the Herculean task of uprooting the ancient superstitions that held vast numbers of people in their toils. To convert priests was generally considered more difficult. While Voltaire hailed clerics like Meslier who had become covert adherents of the new philosophy, ecclesiastical institutions were usually regarded as beyond redemption. The *philosophes* therefore aimed their most violent blasts against the churches of all nations. Since they could not persuade these despoilers of men's reason, they had to fight them. Reluctant to take an unequivocal position against monarchical power, they were less timorous about assailing religious authority, especially when they were allied with the kings who resented the rival strength of the Church. By the eve of the French Revolution new explanations of the nature of good and the origin of evil had infiltrated the literate upper classes of European society. In Catholic countries, particularly after the expulsion of the Jesuits and the temporary dissolution of their order by the Papacy, reformers and philosophical abbés came to control the education of the aristocracy. When the new ideology penetrated to the seats of power, it naturally undermined the spiritual sanctions of the ruling classes and thus helped to bring about the very political upheavals which most of the *philosophes* would have wished to avert.

First among the immediate programs for action suggested by the *philosophes* was religious reform. The practices of existing church establishments were attacked as both unnatural and wicked, unnatural because they taught false doctrine and propagated a belief in the innate sinfulness of man, wicked because they bred cruelty and perpetuated superstition. For enlightened men natural religion was the only true religion, and that meant a religion virtually without theological dogmas or ecclesiastical establishments. Tolerance and a benign morality universally applicable were considered a part of natural religion. Many still clung to the doctrine of the immortality of the soul as an instrument to strengthen men's virtuousness in this life. But they would strip religion of its elaborate ceremonial. The simple worship of God was adequate for the fulfillment of man's religious needs.

To the thinkers of the eighteenth century the greatest evil was not error but superstition. They were certain that through education they could ultimately vanquish ignorance, but prejudice and intolerance, the false mysteries long enshrined in civic and ecclesiastical institutions, and religious fanaticism over matters of no consequence had to be fought tooth and nail. This was perhaps their chief mission.

When the *philosophes* came to examine the prevailing teachings of the church in the light of their newly acquired scientific values, few doctrines could pass muster. There was a tremendous popularization of Biblical criticism by the more extreme anti-clerical writers among them, and the authenticity of the Sacred Books as divine revelation was called into doubt. If two passages in the Bible were not consistent with each other, if one proposition in them was not deducible from another, then by the canon of sound Cartesian reason the absolute veracity of the Bible could not be sustained. There might be some refuge in a sharp bifurcation of the world into a realm of faith and a realm of reason, but this left a measure of uneasiness among the intellectual faithful, and wholly failed to silence the skeptics. Had the sun really halted in its course at Joshua's command and had Christ actually multiplied the loaves? A belief in miracles could hardly be entertained by those who accepted a popular if somewhat erroneous presentation of the Newtonian system. Today even the devout are less troubled by such problems because the Bible is given an allegorical or, more often, a historical interpretation; but the eighteenth-century *philosophes* asked the orthodox direct and pointed questions and demanded specific answers from religious institutions that still insisted upon holding fast to the literal meaning of every word in the Biblical text.

The great theological debates of the sixteenth and seventeenth centuries had finally wearied men of religious disputation. The very multiplicity of contradictory dogmas among rival religions gave those who had a straightforward faith in science a feeling of certainty and security. In religion there were Scotists, Thomists, Calvinists, Jansenists, and a motley agglomeration of sects, but there were no sects in geometry, remarked Voltaire. Of course the scientists occasionally waged titanic battles over their personal and philosophical differences. But Newton and Leibniz fought about who had first invented the calculus, not about the truth of the calculus itself.

Though the *philosophes* generally shrank from attacking the fundamental principles of the dynastic state, they turned their critical faculties upon some aspects of its administration. Appraising the judicial system, they found that most of the laws were customary, not written; vague and confusing, rather than clear and distinct; harsh and cruel, as well as irrational. The natural rights of man forbade punishments that were useless, that did not serve as deterrents, that were simply exercises in vengeance, or that had a purely religious significance and were based upon the identification of crime with sin. In his little work on crimes and punishments the Italian Beccaria made a passionate plea for the abolition of torture and called for a legal system that would make the punishment fit the crime. "Cold cruelty" was his description of the existing procedures. Advocating leniency, mitigation of the terrible punishments inflicted upon criminals in the European world, the eighteenth-century *philosophes* achieved an immediate if limited success.

The right of equality before the law, for nobles and commoners alike, lay at the heart of the agitation for political reform. When Voltaire was beaten up by retainers of the aristocratic Rohan he had to flee to England lest a worse fate overtake him. In the great lycées of Paris a plebeian dared not strike a noble who sat with him on the same school bench. The *philosophes* were perhaps less preoccupied with the precise form of government—though there was a plentiful literature comparing the relative merits of democracy, aristocracy, and monarchy—than they were with establishing the rule of law, not of men, irrespective of the constitutional theory of a particular state. They worried less about the institutional details of administration than they did about the principle of equal justice for all.

When the *philosophes* directed their attention to the governmental organization of society they saw remnants of feudal law and practice suffocating human initiative, blocking social mobility, and stifling free expression. Custom prevented a man from adopting a new trade. Intricate feudal regulations restricted the movement of grain from one province to another, so that surfeit in one spot where crops were successful could exist with famine in a neighboring area within the same kingdom. Serfs were still bound to the land, particularly in Central and Eastern Europe. Productive industry was disdained, and if a French noble engaged in it he suffered disparagement, loss of status. The *philosophes* demanded liberty of occupational choice and freedom to travel, which would allow artisans to migrate to new lands where better opportunities might await them. They pled for the freedom to purchase and own property outright without becoming embroiled in a web of dues and dependencies which no longer answered any conceivable social need. Often the "freedom" they extolled in their books and pamphlets was economic freedom to build new industries in despite of guild and dynastic state prohibitions. In the economic world they demanded that each individual be allowed to act from self-interest which, they supposed, would ultimately result in a harmony of economic interests.

A cornerstone of the philosophic program was a demand for open expression of ideas without risk of prosecution. It was an article of faith with them that the dissemination of truths through books and newspapers would ultimately bring about the triumph of reason. Hence the unflagging battles for free speech and a free press waged by Montesquieu and by Voltaire. In England and America more advanced opinion added a plea for the right of free assembly.

The struggle to end the power of the state over the promulgation of ideas, to curtail the censorship, should be set against its historical background. After condemnation by the theological faculty of the Sorbonne, major works of the *philosophes* were burned by the public hangman in a formal ceremony in Paris. Baron d'Holbach and others of the philosophical coterie had to make complicated arrangements to print their books anonymously in Amsterdam and then to smuggle them into France. Even in more tolerant England, bishops of the Episcopal Church could exert pressure on wayward authors, forcing them to resort to circumlocutions whose real meaning only those "in the know" could understand. In more backward Italy anti-clerical writers like Pietro Giannone became martyrs for their ideas and languished in jail for years.

Many *philosophes* believed that the church and the state should be separated absolutely. They expected the church to become a mere institute of moral teaching, or they wished strictly to limit its province and its influence to the religious sphere of life. In this field the enlightened despots danced a minuet with the *philosophes*. The rulers of the dynastic state and the intellectuals could make common cause against the church because both favored the clear-cut subordination of the spiritual to the temporal power. Most of the *philosophes* also would have preferred to see a moral, secular education entirely independent of religion. Only rarely did they insist upon destroying the church or denying its right to teach theology.

In general, the moral and political position of the eighteenth-century intellectuals is identified with what David Hume called the "middling' way. Their ideal human type was the stoical Christian gentleman, with perhaps more emphasis on the gentleman than the Christian. They preached moderation, leniency, and a commitment to pleasure, but without excess. While they decried asceticism, continence rather than luxury was their ideal style of life. Few of them were popular democrats and even fewer favored absolute equality in the distribution of property; Morelly's communist principles were an exception. Neither were they atheists, except of course for the circle of Baron d'Holbach. In sum, they believed in free enterprise, Deism, and the reign of a system of law that would safeguard the liberty and security of all citizens from arbitrary and capricious acts.

If the reform program of the *philosophes* were put into effect, would it make man happy? Most of them would have answered "Not immediately." To call this the age of reason is in a sense misleading: it was a period when there was a *quest* for reason. The *philosophes* were all too aware that darkness and superstition still held sway over vast areas of the European continent, let alone the unexplored parts of the world. But there was a reassuring confidence that man was rising again, and they took comfort in a roseate view of the future. The idea of progress has its origins in Christian and in

Renaissance thought, but it culminates in a late eighteenth-century hope. The *philosophes* had a vision of worldly redemption, of an earthly paradise equivalent to the heaven of the Christians. It is perhaps best expressed by the Marquis de Condorcet in his sketch of universal history. There he foresaw a time, which he called the Tenth Epoch, when men would devote themselves only to rational knowledge and science, after science had already eradicated all superstitions from the world. Moral sciences, using the same techniques as the physical sciences, would discover laws applicable to the taming and control of man's own nature. When laws of behavior were formulated Condorcet felt certain they would immediately be enforced with the same alacrity as new technological improvements were adopted. The sick society, the society of unreason, would be cured by scientific laws. Man would become moral because science would teach him to be so. Progress in medicine would result in greater longevity. Progress in the knowledge of agriculture would increase the food supply. Ultimately all crime would end because crime was essentially a disease and new laws of science would know how to eradicate it. Acquired moral characteristics would be inherited, thus guaranteeing the biological transmission of moral progress. War would cease because it would be proved contrary to the rational rules of social science. Condorcet described the Atlantic community—consisting of France, England, and the United States—as living in the forefront of world civilization. All other societies were moving up to their plane of physical, intellectual, and moral achievement. But far from being static this vanguard of world civilization was forging ever further ahead, pulling the rest of mankind along with it. Ultimately, Condorcet believed, all great inequalities among nations, as well as within the nations, would be leveled. In a world society slavery and the dependency of peoples under colonial power would be abolished, and from then on, an indefinite, never-ending progress of the species was assured.

But if all this was for the future, why should men labor for it? Why should men in this generation endure sacrifices for posterity? In reply Condorcet developed the idea of worldly immortality, eternal life in the memory of mankind, as the reward of those who worked for the benefit of humanity. In the *Encyclopédie* Diderot had already approached the same point of view. A new moral value system was being established. Men were to be judged not only by the good they did for their own generation, but by what they accomplished for all future generations. And those who participated in the crusade of progress lived in their imaginations as if the utopia of future happiness had already come true.

The excerpts that follow present a selection of eighteenth-century moral, social, and political opinion. There is a sampling of views on science and reason, religion and superstition, the concept of human nature, the state, and the administration of justice. Finally a section on the philosophy of history epitomizes the outlook of the age on the historical process and the final goal of mankind. The passages chosen are, with a few exceptions, either the original English versions or translations made from the French, German, and Italian in the eighteenth century. Intellectual currents in this period moved easily back and forth across the Channel. It was far more common for the French and English intellectuals to influence their counterparts east of the Rhine than to be affected by the German writings. There is a natural concentration of selections from France, England, Germany (though there is one example from Italy); Spain was intellectually dormant except for late eighteenth-century echoes of French ideas.

The use of eighteenth-century translations has both advantages and drawbacks. On the one hand eighteenth-century English usage is somewhat different from our contemporary one and this may require a certain caution—and occasional resort to a dictionary—on the part of the reader. There are vagaries of spelling and punctuation. On the other hand, vigorous eighteenth-century translation comes closer to preserving the spirit of the original texts, with their inimitable ironies and ambiguities, than would a revamping in present-day terminology.

There would be some justification for beginning this collection with the major thinkers of the second half of the seventeenth century. Since its primary purpose, however, is to communicate Enlightenment ideas at the height of their triumph rather than in their initial stages, we move directly into the middle of the fray. A caveat: the choices lean very heavily in the direction of the *new* ideas, and there is no attempt to represent conservative opinion of the period, which would inevitably run along traditional religious

and philosophical paths. We begin with Voltaire's popular transmission to the Continent in 1733 of "advanced" English ideas on
science and morals, and we end with the proclamation of the idea
of progress, the valedictory of eighteenth-century thought. The philosophical movement probably reached its climax somewhere in the
1760's. By the time the French Revolution broke out, these ideas
had become part and parcel of every up-to-date intellectual's bag-
gage, and they were important equipment for the political action
of the Revolution.

It is to be hoped that the reader will gain some feeling for the
peculiar rhetoric and bombast of the Age of Enlightenment, its
self-assurance and its sense of triumph. If there is at the present
time a tendency to make light of the cocksureness of the *philosophes,* it may be worthwhile to bear in mind that many of the
ideals for which they fought are now taken for granted, and that
in their day European society was corroded by evils we would not
conceive of tolerating in our own world (we have of course acquired other evils). These men were among the great revealers of
mankind. One does not have to believe in their myth of the state
of nature, or even in their utopia of future perfection, to be moved
by the vigor and power of their plea for humanity and for the
rights of man.

Part One

🌸 REASON & SCIENCE

1. Voltaire: Science in England

François Marie Arouet de Voltaire used his descriptions of
English religious tolerance, science, and free government to
condemn by implication French absolutism and the scholastic
philosophy of the Church. His idealization of England and the
"new ideas" may be compared to the report of a sympathetic
twentieth-century intellectual on the morrow of the Russian
Revolution. The excerpts from letters XII through XV of the
Letters Concerning the English Nation discuss with enthusiasm
the work of three English heroes of the Enlightenment: Francis
Bacon, John Locke, and Isaac Newton. Voltaire clearly sides
with Newton against the Cartesians. The work appeared in
English (1733) before it was published in French. We use the
Glasgow, 1766 edition.

Of The Lord Bacon

Not long since, the trite and frivolous question following was debated in a very polite and learned company, viz. who
was the greatest man, Caesar, Alexander, Tamerlane, Cromwell, &c.
Some body answered, that Sir Isaac Newton excelled them all.
The gentleman's assertion was very just; for if true greatness consists in having received from heaven a mighty genius, and having

employed it to enlighten our own minds and that of others; a man like Sir Isaac Newton, whose equal is hardly found in a thousand years, is the truly great man. And those politicians and conquerors (and all ages produce some) were generally so many illustrious wicked men. That man claims our respect, who commands over the minds of the rest of the world by the force of truth, not those who enslave their fellow-creatures; he who is acquainted with the universe, not they who deface it.

Since therefore you desire me to give you an account of the famous personages which England has given birth to, I shall begin with lord Bacon, Mr. Locke, Sir Isaac Newton, &c. afterwards the warriors and ministers of state shall come in their order.

The lord Bacon was not yet acquainted with nature, but then he knew, and pointed out, the several paths that lead to it. He had despised in his younger years the thing called philosophy in the universities; and did all that lay in his power to prevent those societies of men, instituted to improve human reason, from depraving it by their quiddities, their horrors of the vacuum, their substantial forms, and all those impertinent terms which not only ignorance had rendered venerable, but which had been made sacred, by their being ridiculously blended with religion.

In a word, no one, before the lord Bacon, was acquainted with experimental philosophy, nor with the several physical experiments which have been made since his time. Scarce one of them but is hinted at in his work, and he himself had made several. He made a kind of pneumatic engine, by which he guessed the elasticity of the air. He approached, on all sides as it were, to the discovery of its weight, and had very near attained it; but, some time after, Toricelli seized upon this truth. In a little time experimental philosophy began to be cultivated on a sudden in most parts of Europe. It was a hidden treasure which the lord Bacon had some notion of, and which all the philosophers, encouraged by his promises, endeavoured to dig up.

But that which surprized me most, was to read in his work, in express terms, the new attraction, the invention of which is ascribed to Sir Isaac Newton.

We must search, says lord Bacon, whether there may not be a kind of magnetic power, which operates between the earth and heavy bodies, between the moon and the ocean, between the planets, &c. In another place he says, either heavy bodies must be carried towards the center of the earth, or must be reciprocally attracted by it; and in the latter case it is evident, that the nearer bodies, in their falling, draw towards the earth, the stronger they will attract one another. We must, says he, make an experiment, to see whether the same clock will go faster on the top of a mountain or at the bottom of a mine; whether the strength of the weights decreases on the mountain, and increases in the mine. It is probable, that the earth has a true attractive power.

This fore-runner in philosophy was also an elegant writer, an historian, and a wit.

His moral essays are greatly esteemed, but they were drawn up in the view of instructing rather than of pleasing; and as they are not a satire upon mankind, like Rochefoucault's maxims, nor written upon a sceptical plan, like Montagne's essays, they are not so much read as these two ingenious authors.

Of Mr. Locke

Perhaps no man ever had a more judicious, or more methodical genius, or was a more acute logician, than Mr. Locke; and yet he was not deeply skilled in the mathematics. This great man could never subject himself to the tedious fatigue of calculations, nor to the dry pursuit of mathematical truths, which do not at first present any sensible objects to the mind; and no one has given better proofs than he, that it is possible for a man to have a geometrical head, without the assistance of geometry. Before his time, several great philosophers had declared, in the most positive terms, what the soul of man is; but as these absolutely knew nothing about it, they might very well be allowed to differ entirely in opinion from one another.

Such a multitude of reasoners having written the romance of the soul, a sage at last arose, who gave, with an air of the greatest modesty, the history of it. Mr. Locke has displayed the human soul, in the same manner as an excellent anatomist explains the springs of the human body. He everywhere takes the light of physics for his guide. He sometimes presumes to speak affirmatively, but then he presumes also to doubt. Instead of concluding at once what we know not, he examines gradually what we would know. He takes an infant at the instant of his birth; he traces, step by step, the progress of his understanding; examines what thing he has in common with beasts, and what he possesses above them. Above all he consults himself; the being conscious that he himself thinks.

I shall leave, says he, to those who know more of this matter than myself, the examining whether the soul exists before or after the organization of our bodies. But I confess that it is my lot to be animated with one of those heavy souls which do not think always; and I am even so unhappy as not to conceive, that it is more necessary the soul should think perpetually, than that bodies should be for ever in motion.

With regard to myself, I shall boast that I have the honour to be as stupid in this particular as Mr. Locke. No one shall ever make me believe, that I think always; and I am as little inclined as he could be, to fancy that some weeks after I was conceived, I was a very learned soul; knowing at that time a thousand things which I forgot at my birth; and possessing when in the womb, (although to no manner of purpose,) knowledge which I lost the instant I had occasion for it; and which I have never since been able to recover perfectly.

Mr. Locke after having destroyed innate ideas; after having fully renounced the vanity of believing that we think always; after having laid down, from the most solid principles, that ideas enter the mind through the senses; having examined our simple and complex ideas; having traced the human mind through its several operations; having shewed that all the languages in the world are imperfect, and the great abuse that is made of words every moment; he at last comes to consider the extent or rather the narrow limits of human knowledge. It was in this chapter he presumed to advance, but very modestly, the following words, "We shall, perhaps, never be capable of knowing, whether a being, purely material, thinks or not." This sage assertion was, by more divines than one, looked upon as a scandalous declaration that the soul is material and mortal. Some Englishmen, devout after their way, sounded an alarm.

The superstitious are the same in society as cowards in an army;
they themselves are seized with a panic fear, and communicate it to
others. It was loudly exclaimed, that Mr. Locke intended to destroy
religion; nevertheless religion had nothing to do in the affair, it
being a question purely philosophical, altogether independent of
faith and revelation. Mr. Locke's opponents needed but to examine,
calmly and impartially, whether the declaring that matter can think,
implies a contradiction; and whether God is able to communicate thought to matter. But divines are too apt to begin their declarations with saying, that God is offended when people differ from
them in opinion; in which they too much resemble the bad poets,
who used to declare publickly that Boileau spake irreverently of
Lewis the fourteenth, because he ridiculed their stupid productions.
Bishop Stillingfleet got the reputation of a calm and unprejudiced
divine, because he did not expressly make use of injurious terms
in his dispute with Mr. Locke. That divine entered the lists against
him, but was defeated; for he argued as a schoolman, and Locke as
a philosopher, who was perfectly acquainted with the strong as
well as the weak side of the human mind, and who fought with
weapons whose temper he knew. If I might presume to give my
opinion on so delicate a subject after Mr. Locke, I would say, that
men have long disputed on the nature and the immortality of the
soul. With regard to its immortality, it is impossible to give a demonstration of it, since its nature is still the subject of controversy;
which however must be throughly understood, before a person can
be able to determine whether it be immortal or not. Human reason
is so little able, merely by its own strength, to demonstrate the immortality of the soul, that it was absolutely necessary religion should
reveal it to us. It is of advantage to society in general, that mankind should believe the soul to be immortal; faith commands us to
this; nothing more is required, and the matter is cleared up at once.
But it is otherwise with respect to its nature; it is of little importance to religion, which only requires the soul to be virtuous, what
substance it may be made of. It is a clock which is given us to regulate, but the artist has not told us of what materials the spring of
this clock is composed.

I am a body, and, I think, that is all I know of the matter. Shall
I ascribe to an unknown cause, what I can so easily impute to the

only second cause I am acquainted with? here all the school philosophers interrupt me with their arguments, and declare that there
is only extension and solidity in bodies, and that there they can
have nothing but motion and figure. Now motion, figure, extension
and solidity cannot form a thought, and consequently the soul cannot be matter. All this, so often repeated, mighty series of reasoning
amounts to no more than this; I am absolutely ignorant what matter is; I guess, but imperfectly, some properties of it; now, I absolutely cannot tell whether these properties may be joined to
thought. As I therefore knew nothing, I maintain positively that
matter cannot think. In this manner do the schools reason.

Mr. Locke addressed these gentlemen in the candid, sincere manner following. At least confess yourselves to be as ignorant as I.
Neither your imaginations nor mine are able to comprehend in
what manner a body is susceptible of ideas; and do you conceive
better in what manner a substance of what kind soever, is susceptible of them? as you cannot comprehend either matter or spirit,
why will you presume to assert any thing?

The superstitious man comes afterwards, and declares, that all
those must be burnt for the good of their souls, who so much as suspect that it is possible for the body to think without any foreign
assistance. But what would these people say should they themselves
be proved irreligious? and indeed what man can presume to assert,
without being guilty at the same time of the greatest impiety, that
it is impossible for the Creator to form matter with thought and
sensation? consider, only, I beg you, what a dilemma you bring
yourselves into; you who confine in this manner the power of the
creator. Beasts have the same organs, the same sensations, the same
perceptions as we; they have memory, and combine certain ideas. In
case it was not in the power of God to animate matter, and inform
it with sensation, the consequence would be, either that beasts are
mere machines, or that they have a spiritual soul.

Methinks it is clearly evident that beasts cannot be mere machines, which I prove thus. God has given them the very same organs of sensation as to us: if therefore they have no sensation, God
has created an useless thing; now, according to your own confession,
God does nothing in vain; he therefore did not create so many organs of sensation, merely for them to be uninformed with this

faculty; consequently beasts are not mere machines. Beasts, according to your assertion, cannot be animated with a spiritual soul; you will therefore, in spite of yourself, be reduced to this only assertion, viz. that God has endued the organs of beasts who are mere matter, with the faculties of sensation and perception, which you call instinct in them. But why may not God, if he pleases, communicate to our more delicate organs that faculty of feeling, perceiving, and thinking, which we call human reason? to whatever side you turn, you are forced to acknowledge your own igonorance, and the boundless power of the Creator. Exclaim therefore no more against the sage, the modest philosophy of Mr. Locke, which, so far from interfereing with religion, would be of use to demonstrate the truth of it, in case religion wanted any such support, for what philosophy can be of a more religious nature than that, which affirming nothing but what it conceives clearly, and conscious of its own weakness, declares that we must always have recourse to God in our examining of the first principles.

Besides, we must not be apprehensive, that any philosophical opinion will ever prejudice the religion of a country. Though our demonstrations clash directly with our mysteries, that is nothing to the purpose, for the latter are not less revered upon that account by our Christian philosophers, who know very well that the objects of reason and those of faith are of a very different nature. Philosophers will never form a religious sect, the reason of which is, their writings are not calculated for the vulgar, and they themselves are free from enthusiasm. If we divide mankind into twenty parts, it will be found that nineteen of these consist of persons employed in manual labour, who will never know that such a man as Mr. Locke existed.

In the remaining twentieth part, how few are readers! and among such as are so, twenty amuse themselves with romances to one who studies philosophy. The thinking part of mankind are confined to a very small number, and those will never disturb the peace and tranquility of the world.

Neither Monta[i]gne, Locke, Bayle, Spinoza, Hobbes, the lord Shaft[e]sbury, Collins nor Toland, lighted up the firebrand of discord in their countries; this has generally been the work of divines, who, being at first puffed up with the ambition of becoming chiefs of a sect, soon grew very desirous of being at the head of a party.

But what do I say? all the works of the modern philosophers put together will never make so much noise as even the dispute which
arose among the Franciscans, merely about the fashion of their
sleeves and of their cowls.

Of Attraction

The discoveries, which gained Sir Isaac Newton so universal a reputation, relate to the system of the world, to light, to geometrical infinities, and lastly to chronology, with which he used to
amuse himself after the fatigue of his severer studies.

I will now acquaint you (without prolixity if possible) with the
few things I have been able to comprehend of all these sublime
ideas. With regard to the system of our world, disputes were a long
time maintained, on the cause that turns the planets, and keeps
them in their orbits; and on those causes which make all bodies
here below descend towards the surface of the earth.

The system of Des Cartes, explained and improved since his time,
seemed to give a plausible reason for all those phaenomena; and
this reason seemed more just, as it is simple, and intelligible to all
capacities. But in philosophy a student ought to doubt of the things
he fancies he understands too easily, as much as of those he does not
understand.

This power of gravitation acts proportionably to the quantity of
matter in bodies, a truth which Sir Isaac has demonstrated by experiments. This new discovery has been of use to shew, that the sun
(the center of the planetary system) attracts them all in a direct
ratio of their quantity of matter combined with their nearness.
From hence Sir Isaac, rising by degrees to discoveries which seemed
not to be formed for the human mind, is bold enough to compute
the quantity of matter contained in the sun and in every planet;
and in this manner shews, from the simple law of mechanics, that
every celestial globe ought necessarily to be where it is placed.

His bare principle of the laws of gravitation accounts for all the
apparent inequalities in the course of the celestial globes. The varia-
tions of the moon are a necessary consequence of those laws.

Moreover the reason is evidently seen why the nodes of the moon perform their revolutions in nineteen years, and those of the earth in about twenty six thousand. The several appearances observed in the tides are also a very simple effect of this attraction. The proximity of the moon when at the full, and when it is new, and its distance in the quadratures or quarters combined with the action of the sun, exhibit a sensible reason why the ocean swells and sinks.

This is attraction, the great spring by which all nature is moved. Sir Isaac Newton, after having demonstrated the existence of this principle, plainly foresaw that its very name would offend; and therefore this philosopher in more places than one of his books, gives the reader some caution about it. He bids him beware of confounding this name with what the ancients called occult qualities; but to be satisfied with knowing that there is in all bodies a central force which acts to the utmost limits of the universe, according to invariable laws of mechanics.

Give me leave once more to introduce Sir Isaac speaking; shall he not be allowed to say, my case and that of the ancients is very different? These saw, for instance, water ascend in pumps, and said, the water rises because it abhors a *vacuum*. But with regard to myself, I am in the case of a man who should have first observed that water ascends in pumps, but should leave others to explain the cause of this effect. The anatomist who first declared, that the motion of the arm is owing to the contraction of the muscles, taught mankind an indisputable truth; but are they less obliged to him because he did not know the reason why the muscles contract? The cause of the elasticity of the air is unknown, but he who first discovered this spring performed a very signal service to natural philosophy. The spring that I discovered was more hidden and more universal, and for that very reason mankind ought to thank me the more. I have discovered a new property of matter, one of the secrets of the Creator; and have calculated and discovered the effects of it. After this shall people quarrel with me about the name I gave it?

2. Rousseau: The Folly of Vain Learning

What is known as Jean-Jacques Rousseau's *Discourse on the Arts and Sciences* was a paradoxical challenge to the rationalist *philosophes*—delivered by one of their friends at a time when the movement was just beginning to gain momentum. His plea was for a recognition of the superiority of nature over science, of the perfection of man's inner being over his outward achievement. It would be repeated by Rousseau for almost four decades in a wide variety of writings—novels, essays, treatises—composed in an intoxicating, dramatic style. He is one of the most enigmatic figures of the Enlightenment, eminently quotable on virtually any moral, political, and social problem. His rhetoric exerted a powerful intellectual and emotional influence on the French Revolution. Here follow the opening pages of the first English translation by W. Bowyer (London, 1751). Its full title was *The Discourse which Carried the Praemium at the Academy of Dijon, in MDCCL. On this Question, Propos'd by the said Academy, Whether the Re-establishment of Arts and Sciences has contributed to the refining of Manners. By a Citizen of Geneva.*

"Has the re-establishment of arts and sciences contributed to purge or corrupt our manners?" This is the question in debate; which side shall I take, Gentlemen? That which becomes an honest man who knows nothing, and is not asham'd to own it.

I foresee the difficulty of appropriating what I have to say to the tribunal I appear before. How shall I dare to depreciate the sciences in the presence of one of the most learned Assemblies in *Europe*? Run out into the praises of ignorance in the midst of a celebrated Academy; or reconcile my disdain for study with the respect due to the truly learned? I saw these difficulties, but was not deterr'd by them. 'Tis not the Sciences, said I to myself, that I attack; 'tis the

26

Cause of Virtue that I support before virtuous judges; honour, honesty, and probity, are dearer to good men than erudition to even the learned—What then have I to dread? The penetration of the honourable assembly, before whom I speak, I own, is to be fear'd: but it is more for the construction of the oration, than for the sentiments of the orator; equitable sovereigns never hesitate to condemn themselves in all doubtful cases; and the happiest situation for a just cause is, to be admitted to a defence where its upright and learned adversary is judge.—If to this motive, which has encouraged me, another be wanting, let it be, that after having, to the best of my skill, defended the truth, whatever my success may be, there is a prize which cannot fail me, I shall find it at the bottom of my own heart.

It is a beautiful noble prospect to view man, as it were, rising again from nothing by his own efforts; dissipating, by the light of his reason, all the thick clouds in which nature had involv'd him; mounting above himself: soaring in thought even to the celestial regions; marching like the sun, with giant strides around the vast universe; and, what is still grander and more wonderful, re-entering into himself to study man, to dive into his nature, his duties, his end. All these wonders have been renew'd within these few last generations.

Europe was relapsed into the barbarity of the first ages; the inhabitants of that part of the world, which now makes so great a figure in knowledge, were plung'd, some centuries ago, into a state which was worse than utter ignorance. A certain school jargon, more despicable than ignorance itself, had usurp'd the name of knowledge, and opposed an almost invincible obstacle to its restoration, a revolution became necessary to lead people back into common sense: and it came at last from the corner of the world the least suspected; it was the stupid Mussulman, the sworn enemy to letters, that caus'd their revival among us. The fall of *Constantine's* throne brought the relicks of antient *Greece* into *Italy; France* in her turn was enrich'd by the precious spoils; the sciences soon follow'd letters, and the art of thinking was join'd to that of writing: this gradation seems strange, but it is perhaps but too natural; and men began to feel the principal advantage accruing from the love of the Muses, that of rendering mankind more sociable, by inspiring the thirst of pleasing each other by works worthy of mutual approbation.

There are necessaries for the mind, as well as for the body; these are the foundation of society, those its ornament. Whilst the government and laws provide for the safety and well-being of a people assembled; the sciences, letters, and arts, less arbitrary, tho' perhaps more powerful, strow garlands of flowers on their iron fetters, smother those sentiments of original liberty, with which they would seem to have been born, make them in love with their slavery, and so form, what we call, a polish'd nation. Necessity rais'd thrones; and the arts and sciences support them.—Ye powers of the earth cherish all talents, and protect those who cultivate them: go on ye polish'd nations, improve, advance and enlarge them: to them, ye happy slaves, you owe that delicacy of taste you boast of, that sweetness of character, and that urbanity of manners, which renders your civil commerce so easy, so flowing, and so engaging: in a word, the appearance of every virtue without possessing one.

'Twas by these kind of accomplishments, which become much the more amiable for their affectation of not appearing, that *Athens* and *Rome* were formerly so renown'd in those boasted days of their magnificence and glory: and it is, no doubt, for the same reason that our days and our kingdom bear the sway from all ages and all nations;—An air of philosophy without pedantry, an address that is natural and yet engaging, equally distant from northern rusticity and *Italian* mimickry: those are the fruits produced by the arts and sciences which are ripened and brought to perfection by the commerce of the world.

What a happiness it would be to live amongst us, if our exterior appearance were always the true representation of our hearts; if our decency were virtue, if our maxims were the rules of our actions, if true philosophy were inseparably annex'd to the title of philosopher! But so many good qualities are not always found together, and virtue seldom appears in such pomp and state. Dress will set forth the man of fortune, and elegance the man of taste; but the wholesome robust man is known by other marks. The strength and vigour of body are found under the coarse homely coverings of the labouring peasant, not under the courtier's embroidery. So all ornaments are strangers to virtue, which is the strength and vigour of the soul: the honest man is a champion who wrestles stark naked; he disdains all those vile accoutrements which prove only incumbrances, that marr his natural force and activity, and were only first invented to hide some defect or deformity.

Before art had new moulded our behaviours, and taught our passions to talk an affected language, our manners were indeed rustick, but sincere and natural; and the difference of our behaviours in an instant distinguished our characters.—'Tis true, that human nature was not then any wise better in the main than now: but man found a security in the ease with which he could dive into the thoughts of man; and this advantage, on which we seem to set no price, exempted them from many vices.

In these our days the art of pleasing is by subtil researches, and finery of taste, reduced to certain principles; insomuch that a vile deceitful uniformity runs thro' our whole system of manners: as if all our constitutions, all our minds had been cast in one and the same mold.—Politeness constantly requires, civility commands; we always follow customs, never our particular inclinations: no one, now a-days, dares to appear what he really is; and in this perpetual constraint, the individuals who compose the congregation called society, being put into the same circumstances, will one and all act in the same manner, unless some more powerful motive intervene. Shall we then never rightly know the man we converse with? Must we, in order to distinguish the sincere friend, wait for grand occasions, I mean till it be too late; for it is for grand occasions that it were of the highest consequence to know him before-hand.

What a train of vices attend this uncertainty? Friendships are insincere, esteem is not real, and confidence is ill founded; suspicions, jealousies, fears, coolnesses, reserve, hatred, and treasons, are hid under the uniform veil of perfidious politeness, under that boasted civility which we owe to the vast discoveries of our age. 'Tis true, no one will swear by the name of the Omnipotent Master of the universe, 'tis not polite; but he shall be blasphemed in speeches and writings, without offending our scrupulous ears. No one will boast of his own merit, but he will run down that of his neighbour. No one will outrageously insult his enemy, but he will slyly calumniate him; national hatreds will be quench'd, but it will be in the love of our country. The place of despised ignorance will be occupied by a more despicable Pyrrhonism. Some excesses indeed will be proscribed, some vices dishonoured; but others will be adorn'd with the dress and name of virtues, which if we have not, we must affect to have. Let who will boast of the sobriety of the sages of our days; for my own part I can perceive nothing but a refinement of intemperance, as unworthy of my approbation as is their artificial simplicity.

Such is the purity which our manners have acquired. Thus we are become great and good. Let arts, letters, and sciences now claim what belongs to them in this noble and salutary work.—I shall only add one reflection; if the inhabitant of some far distant region would form an idea of our European manners on the condition in which the sciences are amongst us, on the perfection of our arts, on the decency of our publick diversions, on the politeness of our behaviour, on the affability of our conversations, on our perpetual demonstrations of good-will to each other, and on that tumultuous concourse of men of all ages, of all conditions, who, from sun rise to sun set, seem eternally employ'd in obliging one another; would not this stranger conclude our manners to be the exact reverse of what they really are? Where we see no effect, 'tis in vain to seek for a cause; but here the effect is visible, the depravation palpable; our minds have been corrupted in proportion as our arts and sciences have made advances toward their perfection.—Shall we say that this is a misfortune particular to our times? No, gentlemen, the evils arising from our vain curiosity are as old as the world. The flow and ebb of the sea are not more regularly guided by the moon's course, than our manners and probity by that of the arts and sciences. We see virtue flying on one side, as their lights rise on the other of our horizon: and the same phaenomenon has been observed in all times and in all places.

Let us view *Egypt,* the original school of the universe, that beautiful, fertile and cloudless climate, that celebrated country, whence *Sesostris* formerly issued to conquer the world. *Egypt* becomes the mother of philosophy and arts, but soon after, the prey of *Cambyses,* and presently that of the *Greeks,* the *Romans,* the *Arabs,* and at last that of the *Turks.*

See *Greece,* formerly peopled by heroes who twice conquer'd *Asia,* once at *Troy,* and again at their own doors. Learning, in her infancy, had not yet corrupted the hearts of her inhabitants; but the progress of sciences, the dissolution of manners, and the *Macedonian* yoke, invaded her, as I may say, on the heels of one another: then poor *Greece*, still learned, still voluptuous, still a slave, knew no other revolutions but the frequent changes of her masters; nor could all the eloquence of *Demosthenes* revive a body, which luxury and the arts had totally enervated.

It was in the time of *Ennius*, in that of *Terence*, that *Rome*, which had been founded by a shepherd and made famous by Ploughmen, began to degenerate; but after, when the *Ovids*, the *Catullus's*, the *Martials*, and that crowd of obscene authors, whose names alone are enough to shock common modesty, when they appear'd, *Rome*, from being the temple of virtue, became the theatre of wickedness, the aversion of nations, and the scoff of *Barbarians*. That great capital of the world falls herself under the same captivity which she so often impos'd on other nations; and the time of her fall was the eve of that day on which she bestow'd on one of her citizens the title of sole arbiter of *fine taste*. What shall I say of that metropolis of the eastern empire, which by its situation would seem to have had a right of command over the whole world? That refuge of arts and sciences, after they had been proscrib'd by the rest of *Europe* perhaps more through wisdom than barbarity? All that render corruption and debauchery shameful, that can blacken treasons, murders, and poisonings; all the concourse of the most atrocious crimes seem combin'd together to form the history of *Constantinople;* and yet that is the pure source whence have flow'd those floods of light and knowledge so boasted of in our days.

But what need we recur to those past ages for proofs of this truth whilst we have living evidences subsisting before our eyes? We have in *Asia* an immense track of land, where learning flourishes, and is the best qualification for filling the first and greatest places, employments, and dignities of the state. If the sciences really better'd manners, if they taught man to spill his blood for his country, if they heighten'd his courage; the inhabitants of *China* ought to be wise, free, and invincible.—But if they are tainted with every vice, familiar with every crime; if neither the skill of their magistrates, nor the pretended wisdom of their laws, nor the vast multitude of people inhabiting that great extent of empire, could protect or defend them from the yoke of an ignorant *Barbarian Tartar,* of what use was all their art, all their skill, all their learning? What was the benefit accruing from all the respect with which they were adorn'd and honour'd? unless that *China* is peopled with slaves and cheats.—Let us set, in opposition to these frightful pictures, that of those few countries, who, having the good fortune to have been preserv'd from the contagion of vain knowledge, have procur'd, by their virtue, happiness for themselves, and have prov'd the great examples of all other nations. Such were the first *Persians,* a very singular nation, who made virtue their study, as we do sciences; who subdued *Asia* with so much ease, and who alone had the glory of having the history of their institutions pass for a philosophical romance: such were the *Scythians,* of whom we have such magnificent elogiums: such the *Germans,* whom an able writer, wearied by describing the horrid crimes of an opulent voluptuous learned people, has taken delight to celebrate for their simplicity, their innocence, their virtues.—Such was even *Rome* herself in the times of her poverty and ignorance; and such, in short, appear'd, in our own days, that rude unpolish'd nation so renown'd for courage, which no adversity could abate, and for loyalty, which example could not corrupt.

It was not through stupidity that these preferred the bodily exercises to those of the mind; they knew well enough that idlers in other countries pass'd their whole lives in disputes about the *summum bonum,* about vice and virtue, and that proud reasoners, vainly bestowing praises on themselves, jumbled all other nations under the despicable denomination of *Barbarians:* but they have duly considered their lives and manners, and thence despised their doctrines.

Can we forget that in the very bosom of *Greece* herself there arose a city which became famous thro' a happy ignorance, and the wisdom of her laws? A commonwealth peopled rather by demi-gods than men, so far did their virtue outshine humanity. O *Sparta!* thou proof of the folly of vain learning! whilst all manner of vice, led by the arts and sciences were introduced into *Athens,* whilst a tyrant was busy in picking up the works of the prince of poets, thou wert chasing from thy walls all sciences, all learning, together with their professors.

The success of both was thus distinguished: *Athens* became the mansion of politeness and fine taste, the seat of eloquence and philosophy; the elegance of their buildings corresponded with that of their language. On all sides were seen the marble and animated canvas fresh from the hands of the greatest masters. 'Twas from *Athens* that all those surprizing works, which will for ever be models for all corrupted ages, have sprung. The picture of *Lacedaemon* is not so brilliant. *There,* said all other nations, *there men are born virtuous, the very air of that country seems to inspire virtue.* Nothing remains of that people but the tradition of their heroick actions.

3. Kant: Freedom to Reason

For many historians Immanuel Kant's philosophical system represents the culmination of eighteenth-century thought. His great *Critiques* defined the nature and set the limits of metaphysical and practical reason. *An Answer to the Question, What is Enlightening?* was written for popular consumption in a Berlin monthly (1784). The essay is of particular interest because of Kant's distinction between the exercise of public liberty to reason, which is the duty of all mature men, and private obedience to professional rules and regulations promulgated by traditional bodies. Kant's rather playful assertion that this is an "age of enlightening," but not yet an "enlightened age," should serve to render more nuanced the often stereotyped image of the Königsberg professor and his epoch. We reproduce in full the English translation of *What is Enlightening?* by A. F. M. Willich that appeared in Kant's *Essays and Treatises on Moral, Political and Various Philosophical Subjects* (London, 1798, 1799).

Enlightening is, Man's quitting the nonage occasioned by himself. Nonage or minority is the inability of making use of one's own understanding without the guidance of another. This nonage is *occasioned by one's self*, when the cause of it is not from want of understanding, but of resolution and courage to use one's own understanding without the guidance of another. *Sapere aude!* Have courage to make use of thy own understanding! is therefore the *dictum* of enlightening.

Laziness and cowardice are the causes, why so great a part of mankind, after nature has long freed them from the guidance of others (*naturaliter majorennes*), willingly remain minors as long as they live; and why it is so easy for others, to set themselves up as their guardians. It is convenient to be a minor. If I have a book, which has understanding for me, a curate, who has conscience for me, a physician, who judges of diet for me, etc. I need not give myself any trouble. I have no occasion to think, if I can but pay; others will save me the trouble of that irksome business. Those guardians, who have graciously undertaken the superintendence of mankind, take sufficient care, that by far the greater part of them (and all the fair) shall hold the step to majority, besides the trouble attending it, very dangerous. After these superintendents have first made them as stupid as their domestic animals, and carefully prevented those peaceable creatures from daring to venture a single step beyond the go-cart, in which they are inclosed; they point out to them the danger that threatens them, if they should try to go alone. Indeed this danger is not so very great, for, at the expence of a few falls, they would learn to walk at last; but an example of this sort renders timid, and commonly discourages from all further attempts. It is therefore difficult for every single man to extricate himself from the nonage, which is almost become natural to him. Nay, it is even become agreeable to him, and he is for the present actually incapable of using his own understanding, because he never was allowed to make the trial. Ordinances and formules, the mechanical instruments of a rational use, or rather misuse, of his gifts of nature, are the fetters of an everlasting minority. Whoever shook them off, would take but an uncertain leap over the smallest ditch even, because he is not accustomed to such a free motion. Hence there are but few, who have succeeded to emancipate themselves from nonage by their own labour, and yet to walk firmly.

But it is sooner possible for a nation to enlighten itself; nay, when it has the liberty, it is almost infallible. For a few who think for themselves will always be found, even among the installed guardians of the multitude, who, after they themselves have thrown off the yoke of nonage, will spread about them the spirit of a rational estimation of the proper value and of the vocation of every man to think for himself. It is singular in this, that the public, which was formerly brought under this yoke by them, afterwards compels them themselves to remain under it, when this public is thereto stirred up by some of its guardians, who are themselves totally incapable of enlightening; so pernicious is it to fill with prejudices; as they are revenged at last on those themselves who, or whose predecessors, were their authors. Hence a nation can attain enlightening but slowly. A deliverance from personal despotism, and interested and tyrannical oppression, may perhaps be obtained by a revolution, but never a true reform of the cast of mind; new prejudices will serve, just as well as the old, for leading-strings to the thoughtless multitude.

　To this enlightening however nothing is required but LIBERTY; and indeed the most harmless of all that may be named liberty, to wit, that, to make a *public use* of one's reason in every point. But I hear exclaimed from all sides: *dont reason!* The officer says: dont reason, but exercise! The financier: dont reason, but pay! The clergyman: dont reason, but believe! (Only one master in the world says: *reason,* as much as you please, and on what you please, *but obey!*) Here is everywhere restriction of liberty. But what restriction is a hinderance to enlightening? what not, but even favourable to it?—My answer is this: the *public* use of one's reason must always be free, and that only can bring about enlightening among men; but the *private use* of it may often be very strictly limited, without much hindering the progress of enlightening. By the public use of one's own reason however I understand that, which every one *as a man of letters* makes of it in the eyes of the whole reading world. I name the private use that, which he may make of his reason in a certain *civil post,* or office, intrusted to him. There is necessary to many businesses, which run in with the interest of the commonwealth, a certain mechanism, by means of which some members of the commonwealth must conduct themselves passively merely, in order, by an artificial unison directed by the government to public ends, to be withholden at least from the destruction of these ends. Here indeed it is not allowed to reason; but one must obey. But so far as this part of the machine considers itself at the same time as a member of the whole commonwealth, nay, even of the cosmopolitical society, consequently in the character of a man of letters, who addresses himself by writings to the public in the proper sense; he may by all means reason, without doing any injury thereby to the business, to which he is appointed, partly as a passive member. It would be very hurtful, if an officer, to whom his superiour gives an order, should in actual service reason loudly on the conformity-to-end, or expediency of this order; he must obey. But he, as a man of letters, cannot in justice be hindered from making his observations on the faults of the military service, and from submitting these to the judgment of the public. The citizen cannot refuse to pay the taxes imposed on him; even a forward censure of such taxes, when they are to be paid by him, may be punished as a scandal (which might occasion universal opposition). The very same person, notwithstanding that, does not act contrary to the duty of a citizen, when he, as a man of letters, publishes his thoughts on the unfitness or even the injustice of such imposts. In like manner is a clergyman bound, to deliver himself to his congregation in all points according to the symbol of the church, which he serves; for he was ordained on this condition. But as a man of letters he has full liberty, nay, it is his call, to communicate to the public all his carefully proved and well-meant thoughts on what is faulty in that symbol, and to make his proposals for the better regulation of the affairs of religion and of the church. There is nothing in this, which can be burdensome to the conscience. For, what he teaches pursuant to his office, as agent of the church, he represents as something, in respect of which he has not a free power to teach according to his own sentiments, but he is ordered to propound that according to precept and in the name of another. He may say: our church inculcates this, or that doctrine; these are the arguments it makes use of. He then draws all practical profit to his congregation from ordinances, to which he himself would not subscribe, perhaps with full conviction, to whose propounding however he can bind himself, because it is not quite impossible that truth may lie therein concealed, but at all events nothing is found in them inconsistent at least with the internal religion. For, did he believe to find in them any thing repugnant to this, he could not administer his office with a safe conscience; he must resign it. The use, therefore, which an established teacher or pastor makes of his reason before his hearers, is a *private use* merely; as this is never but a domestic congregation, though ever so great; and in regard to which he, as *a priest,* is not free, and dare not be so, because he executes the commission of another. Whereas, as a man of letters, who speaks by writings to the proper public, namely, the world, consequently the ecclesiastic, in the *public use* of his reason, enjoys an unlimited liberty, to use his own reason and to speak in his own person. For it is an absurdity, which tends to the perpetuating of absurdities, that the guardians of the people (in spiritual things) shall themselves be again in a state of nonage.

But should not a society of clergymen, for instance, a church-assembly, or a reverend class (as the Dutch clergy name themselves) be entitled to bind one another by oath to a certain unalterable symbol, in order to exercise an incessant supreme guardianship over every one of their members and by their means over the people, and even to eternize this? I maintain that that is totally impossible. Such a contract, entered into for the purpose of withholding for ever all farther enlightening from the human species, is absolutely void; and should it be confirmed by the chief power even, by diets of the empire, and by the most solemn treaties of peace. An age cannot league itself, and by oath too, to put the following age into a state, wherein it must be impossible for it to enlarge its knowledge (especially a knowledge so very important), to purge away errors, and in general to make progress in enlightening. That were a crime against human nature, whose original destination consists directly in this progression; and posterity is therefore completely entitled to reject those resolutions, as at once incompetently and presumptuously formed. The test of all that can be finally determined with regard to a nation, lies in the question, Whether a nation itself could institute such a law? This would, as it were, in the expectation of a better, be possible for a determinate short time, with a view to introduce a better order; if at the same time all the citizens, principally the clergy, had the liberty, in the character of men of letters, to make their observations publicly, that is, by writings, on that which is faulty of the present œconomy, but the established order might still continue, till the insight into the nature of these things attained such a degree, that they (the citizens) by uniting their voices (though not of all) could make a proposal to the throne, to take under its protection those congregations, which had united themselves in an altered œconomy of religion according to their conceptions of a better introspection, without however molesting those, who rather chuse to continue with the old. But to unite one's self in a permanent constitution of religion, to be questioned by nobody publicly, even but during the life-time of one man, and thereby, as it were, annihilate a period in the progression of humanity to amendment, to render it fruitless and by that means even detrimental to posterity, is absolutely not allowed. A man may indeed, as to his own person, defer, and even then but for a time, the enlightening in that, which is incumbent on him to know; but to renounce it, let it be for his own person, but still more for posterity, is to violate and to trample on the sacred rights of humanity. But what a nation cannot finally determine with regard to themselves, still less can the monarch determine that finally with regard to the nation; for his legislative dignity rests upon his uniting in his own will the common will of the nation. If he but takes care, that all true or opiniative improvement be consistent with the civil order; as for the rest, he may let his subjects themselves do what they find necessary to be done for the sake of the welfare of their own souls; that does not concern him, but it concerns him to take care that the one shall not violently prevent the other from labouring with all his strength at the determination and furtherance of that welfare. He derogates from his own majesty, when he interferes with the writings, by which his subjects endeavour to perfectionate their insights, and thinks them worthy of the inspection of his government, as well as when he does this from his own profound introspection, where he exposes himself to the exprobration, *Caesar non est supra grammaticos,* as also, and still more, when he humbles his supreme power so far, as to support the ecclesiastic despotism of a few tyrants in his state against his other subjects.

If it is now enquired, do we live at present in an *enlightened* age? The answer is, No, but by all means in an age of *enlightening.* There is still a great deal wanting to men, as things are at present, on the whole, to be in a state, or to be but able to be put in a state, to make a safe and a good use of their own understanding in affairs of religion without the guidance of another. But we have distinct proofs, that the field is now opened for them to labour in freely, and the hinderances of universal enlightening, or of quitting the nonage occasioned by themselves, become by degrees fewer. In this respect the present age is the age of enlightening, or FREDE-RICK'S century.

A prince, who does not think it unworthy of himself to say, that he holds it *duty,* not to prescribe any thing to men in matters of religion, but to allow them full liberty therein, who declines, even the lofty *name of being tolerating,* is himself enlightened, and merits to be esteemed as such by the grateful world and by posterity, a prince, who first freed the human species from nonage, at least on the part of government, and gave them liberty, in all that is an affair of conscience, to use their own reason. Under him could respectable clergymen, in the character of men of letters, without prejudice to the duty of their office, freely expose to the world to be proved their judgments and insights, here and there deviating from the received symbol; and still more every other person, who is limited by no duty of office. This spirit of liberty diffuses itself outwardly also, even where it has to struggle with external impediments of a government misunderstanding itself. For it gives an example to that government, that it needs not, on account of liberty, be under the smallest solicitude for the tranquillity, and union of the commonwealth. Men naturally extricate themselves insensibly from the state of rudeness and barbarity, when invention is not purposely plied to keep them in it.

The stress of the principal point of enlightening, that of men's quitting the nonage occasioned by themselves, I have laid upon *matters of religion* chiefly; because, with regard to arts and sciences, our rulers have no interest in playing the guardian over their subjects; besides, that state of nonage is not only the most pernicious, but the most dishonourable of any. But the way of thinking of a head of the state, who favours enlightening penetrates farther and perspects, That even in regard of his *legislation* there is no danger in allowing his subjects to make a *public* use of their reason, and to lay before the world their thoughts on a better constitution, and even a free and honest criticism of the present; we have an eminent example of this, in which no monarch ever surpassed him, whom we honour.

But only he, who, enlightened himself, is not only not afraid of his shadow, but has at hand a well-disciplined numerous army as a security for the public tranquillity, can say, what a free state dares not risk: *reason as much as you please, and on what you please, but obey!* Thus a strange unexpected course of human affairs presents itself here; so that, when it is contemplated in the gross, almost every thing is paradoxical in it. A greater degree of civil liberty seems advantageous to the liberty of the *spirit of the nation,* and yet places insuperable barriers to it; whereas a degree less of that gives this full scope to extend itself to the utmost of its faculty. When nature has then unfolded under this rough rind the germe, of which she takes the most tender care, namely, the propensity and the call to *thinking freely;* this gradually reacts on the minds of the people (whereby they become by degrees more capable *of the liberty of acting*), and finally, even on the principles of the government, which finds it profitable for itself to treat man, who is now more than a mere *machine,* conformably to his dignity.

Part Two

RELIGION & SUPERSTITION

1. Hume: The Origins of Religion

The origins of religion was a favorite topic of inquiry and debate among the eighteenth-century philosophers. David Hume's subtle, often snide, *Natural History of Religion* is probably the single most important work in the controversy. Denying the doctrine of "primitive monotheism" to which both orthodox believers and rationalist Deists were committed, he formulated a theory of the origins of religion in fear and hope. This essay had a profound effect on the development of a modern psychology of religion.

We use excerpts from two sections entitled "Origin of Polytheism." The essay was first published as one of *Four Dissertations* (London, 1757).

That Polytheism Was the Primary Religion of Men

It appears to me, that if we consider the improvement of human society, from rude beginnings to a state of greater perfection, polytheism or idolatry was, and necessarily must have been, the first and most ancient religion of mankind. This opinion I shall endeavor to confirm by the following arguments.

It is a matter of fact incontestable, that about 1700 years ago all mankind were polytheists. The doubtful and sceptical principles of a few philosophers, or the theism, and that too not entirely pure, of one or two nations, form no objection worth regarding. Behold then the clear testimony of history. The further we mount up into antiquity, the more do we find mankind plunged into polytheism. No marks, no symptoms of any more perfect religion. The most ancient records of the human race still present us with that system as the popular and established creed. The north, the south, the east, the west, give their unanimous testimony to the same fact. What can be opposed to so full an evidence?

As far as writing or history reaches, mankind, in ancient times, appear universally to have been polytheists. Shall we assert, that in more ancient times, before the knowledge of letters, or the discovery of any art or science, men entertained the principles of pure theism? That is, while they were ignorant and barbarous, they discovered truth, but fell into error as soon as they acquired learning and politeness.

But in this assertion you not only contradict all appearance of probability, but also our present experience concerning the principles and opinions of barbarous nations. The savage tribes of America, Africa, and Asia, are all idolaters. Not a single exception to this rule. Insomuch that, were a traveller to transport himself into any unknown region, if he found inhabitants cultivated with arts and science, though even upon that supposition there are odds against their being theists; yet could he not safely, till further inquiry, pronounce any thing on that head: but if he found them ignorant and barbarous, he might beforehand declare them idolaters, and there scarcely is a possibility of his being mistaken.

It seems certain, that, according to the natural progress of human thought, the ignorant multitude must first entertain some grovelling and familiar notion of superior powers, before they stretch their conception to that perfect Being who bestowed order on the whole frame of nature. We may as reasonably imagine, that men inhabited palaces before huts and cottages, or studied geometry before agriculture; as assert that the Deity appeared to them a pure spirit, omniscient, omnipotent, and omnipresent, before he was apprehended to be a powerful, though limited being, with human passions and appetites, limbs and organs. The mind rises gradually, from inferior to superior: by abstracting from what is imperfect, it forms an idea of perfection: and slowly distinguishing the nobler parts of its own frame from the grosser, it learns to transfer only the former, much elevated and refined, to its divinity. Nothing could disturb this natural progress of thought, but some obvious and invincible argument, which might immediately lead the mind into the pure principles of theism, and make it overleap, at one bound, the vast interval which is interposed between the human and the Divine nature. But though I allow, that the order and frame of the universe, when accurately examined, affords such an argument, yet I can never think, that this consideration could have an influence on mankind, when they formed their first rude notions of religion.

The causes of such objects as are quite familiar to us, never strike our attention and curiosity; and however extraordinary or surprising these objects in themselves, they are passed over by the raw and ignorant multitude, without much examination or inquiry. Adam rising at once in Paradise, and in the full perfection of his faculties, would naturally, as represented by Milton, be astonished at the glorious appearances of nature, the heavens, the air, the earth, his own organs and members; and would be led to ask, whence this wonderful scene arose: but a barbarous, necessitous animal (such as a man is on the first origin of society), pressed by such numerous wants and passions, has no leisure to admire the regular face of nature, or make inquiries concerning the cause of those objects to which, from his infancy, he has been gradually accustomed. On the contrary, the more regular and uniform, that is, the more perfect nature appears, the more is he familiarized to it, and the less inclined to scrutinize and examine it. A monstrous birth excites his curiosity, and is deemed a prodigy. It alarms him from its novelty, and immediately sets him a trembling, and sacrificing, and praying. But an animal, complete in all its limbs and organs, is to him an ordinary spectacle, and produces no religious opinion or affection. Ask him whence that animal arose? he will tell you, from the copulation of its parents. And these, whence? From the copulation of theirs. A few removes satisfy his curiosity, and set the objects at such a distance, that he entirely loses sight of them. Imagine not that he will so much as start the question, whence the first animal, much less whence the whole system or united fabric of the universe arose. Or, if you start such a question to him, expect not that he will employ his mind with any anxiety about a subject so remote, so uninteresting, and which so much exceeds the bounds of his capacity.

But further, if men were at first led into the belief of one superior Being, by reasoning from the frame of nature, they could never possibly leave that belief, in order to embrace polytheism; but the same principles of reason which at first produced and diffused over mankind so magnificent an opinion, must be able, with greater facility, to preserve it. The first invention and proof of any doctrine is much more difficult than the supporting and retaining of it.

There is a great difference between historical facts and speculative opinions; nor is the knowledge of the one propagated in the same manner with that of the other. An historical fact, while it passes by oral tradition from eyewitnesses and contemporaries, is disguised in every successive narration, and may at last retain but very small, if any, resemblance of the original truth on which it was founded. The frail memories of men, their love of exaggeration, their supine carelessness; these principles, if not corrected by books and writing, soon pervert the account of historical events; where argument or reasoning has little or no place, nor can ever recall the truth which has once escaped those narrations. It is thus the fables of Hercules, Theseus, Bacchus, are supposed to have been originally founded in true history, corrupted by tradition. But with regard to speculative opinions, the case is far otherwise. If these opinions be founded on arguments so clear and obvious as to carry conviction with the generality of mankind, the same arguments which at first diffused the opinions, will still preserve them in their original purity. If the arguments be more abstruse, and more remote from vulgar apprehension, the opinions will always be confined to a few persons; and as soon as men leave the contemplation of the arguments, the opinions will immediately be lost and be buried in oblivion. Whichever side of this dilemma we take, it must appear impossible that theism could, from reasoning, have been the primary religion of the human race, and have afterwards, by its corruption, given birth to polytheism, and to all the various superstitions of the heathen world. Reason, when obvious, prevents these corruptions: when abstruse, it keeps the principles entirely from the knowledge of the vulgar, who are alone liable to corrupt any principle or opinion.

Origin of Polytheism

If we would, therefore, indulge our curiosity, in inquiring concerning the origin of religion, we must turn our thoughts towards Polytheism, the primitive religion of uninstructed mankind.

Were men led into the apprehension of invisible, intelligent power, by a contemplation of the works of nature, they could never possibly entertain any conception but of one single being, who bestowed existence and order on this vast machine, and adjusted all its parts, according to one regular plan or connected system. For though to persons of a certain turn of mind, it may not appear altogether absurd, that several independent beings, endowed with superior wisdom, might conspire in the contrivance and execution of one regular plan, yet is this a merely arbitrary supposition, which, even if allowed possible, must be confessed neither to be supported by probability nor necessity. All things in the universe are evidently of a piece. Every thing is adjusted to every thing. One design prevails throughout the whole. And this uniformity leads the mind to acknowledge one author; because the conception of different authors, without any distinction of attributes or operations, serves only to give perplexity to the imagination, without bestowing any satisfaction on the understanding. The statue of LAOCOON, as we learn from Pliny, was the work of three artists: but it is certain, that were we not told so, we should never have imagined, that a group of figures cut from one stone, and united in one plan, was not the work and contrivance of one statuary. To ascribe any single effect to the combination of several causes, is not surely a natural and obvious supposition.

On the other hand, if, leaving the works of nature, we trace the footsteps of Invisible Power in the various and contrary events of human life, we are necessarily led into polytheism, and to the acknowledgment of several limited and imperfect deities. Storms and tempests ruin what is nourished by the sun. The sun destroys what is fostered by the moisture of dews and rains. War may be favorable to a nation, whom the inclemency of the seasons afflicts with famine. Sickness and pestilence may depopulate a kingdom, amidst the most profuse plenty. The same nation is not, at the same time, equally successful by sea and by land. And a nation, which now triumphs over its enemies, may anon submit to their more prosperous arms. In short, the conduct of events, or what we call the plan of a particular Providence, is so full of variety and uncertainty, that, if we suppose it immediately ordered by any intelligent beings, we must acknowledge a contrariety in their designs and intentions, a constant combat of opposite powers, and a repentance or change of intention in the same power, from impotence or levity. Each nation has its tutelar deity. Each element is subjected to its invisible power or agent. The province of each god is separate from that of another. Nor are the operations of the same god always certain and invariable. To-day he protects: to-morrow he abandons us. Prayers and sacrifices, rites and ceremonies, well or ill performed, are the sources of his favor or enmity, and produce all the good or ill fortune which are to be found amongst mankind.

We may conclude, therefore, that, in all nations which have embraced polytheism, the first ideas of religion arose, not from a contemplation of the works of nature, but from a concern with regard to the events of life, and from the incessant hopes and fears which actuate the human mind. Accordingly we find, that all idolaters, having separated the provinces of their deities, have recourse to that invisible agent, to whose authority they are immediately subjected, and whose province it is to superintend that course of actions, in which they are, at any time, engaged. Juno is invoked at marriages; Lucina at births. Neptune receives the prayers of seamen; and Mars of warriors. The husbandman cultivates his field under the protection of Ceres; and the merchant acknowledges the authority of Mercury. Each natural event is supposed to be governed by some intelligent agent; and nothing prosperous or adverse can happen in life, which may not be the subject of peculiar prayers or thanksgivings.

It must necessarily, indeed, be allowed, that, in order to carry men's attention beyond the present course of things, or lead them into any inference concerning invisible intelligent power, they must be actuated by some passion which prompts their thought and re-flection, some motive which urges their first inquiry. But what passion shall we here have recourse to, for explaining an effect of such mighty consequence? Not speculative curiosity, surely, or the pure love of truth. That motive is too refined for such gross apprehensions, and would lead men into inquiries concerning the frame of nature, a subject too large and comprehensive for their narrow capacities. No passions, therefore, can be supposed to work upon such barbarians, but the ordinary affections of human life; the anxious concern for happiness, the dread of future misery, the terror of death, the thirst of revenge, the appetite for food and other necessaries. Agitated by hopes and fears of this nature, especially the latter, men scrutinize, with a trembling curiosity, the course of future causes, and examine the various and contrary events of human life. And in this disordered scene, with eyes still more disordered and astonished, they see the first obscure traces of divinity.

We are placed in this world, as in a great theatre, where the true springs and causes of every event are entirely concealed from us; nor have we either sufficient wisdom to foresee, or power to prevent, those ills with which we are continually threatened. We hang in perpetual suspense between life and death, health and sickness, plenty and want, which are distributed amongst the human species by secret and unknown causes, whose operation is oft unexpected, and always unaccountable. These *unknown causes,* then, become the constant object of our hope and fear; and while the passions are kept in perpetual alarm by an anxious expectation of the events, the imagination is equally employed in forming ideas of those powers on which we have so entire a dependence. Could men anatomize nature, according to the most probable, at least the most intelligible philosophy, they would find that these causes are nothing but the particular fabric and structure of the minute parts of their own bodies and of external objects; and that, by a regular and constant machinery, all the events are produced, about which they are so much concerned. But this philosophy exceeds the comprehension of the ignorant multitude, who can only conceive the *unknown causes,* in a general and confused manner; though their imagination, perpetually employed on the same subject, must labor to form some particular and distinct idea of them. The more they consider these causes themselves, and the uncertainty of their operation, the less satisfaction do they meet with in their researches; and, however unwilling, they must at last have abandoned so arduous an attempt, were it not for a propensity in human nature, which leads into a system that gives them some satisfaction.

There is an universal tendency among mankind to conceive all beings like themselves, and to transfer to every object those qualities with which they are familiarly acquainted, and of which they are intimately conscious. We find human faces in the moon, armies in the clouds; and, by a natural propensity, if not corrected by experience and reflection, ascribe malice or good-will to every thing that hurts or pleases us. Hence the frequency and beauty of the *prosopopœia* in poetry, where trees, mountains, and streams, are personified, and the inanimate parts of nature acquire sentiment and passion. And though these poetical figures and expressions gain not on the belief, they may serve, at least, to prove a certain tendency in the imagination, without which they could neither be beautiful nor natural. Nor is a river-god or hamadryad always taken for a mere poetical or imaginary personage, but may sometimes enter into the real creed of the ignorant vulgar; while each grove or field is represented as possessed of a particular *genius* or invisible power, which inhabits and protects it. Nay, philosophers cannot entirely exempt themselves from this natural frailty; but have oft ascribed to inanimate matter the horror of a *vacuum,* sympathies, antipathies, and other affections of human nature. The absurdity is not less, while we cast our eyes upwards; and, transferring, as is too usual, human passions and infirmities to the Deity, represent him as jealous and revengeful, capricious and partial, and, in short, a wicked and foolish man in every respect but his superior power and authority. No wonder, then, that mankind, being placed in such an absolute ignorance of causes, and being at the same time so anxious concerning their future fortune, should immediately acknowledge a dependence on invisible powers, possessed of sentiment and intelligence. The *unknown causes* which continually employ their thought, appearing always in the same aspect, are all apprehended to be of the same kind or species. Nor is it long before we ascribe to them thought, and reason, and passion, and sometimes even the limbs and figures of men, in order to bring them nearer to a resemblance with ourselves.

In proportion as any man's course of life is governed by accident, we always find that he increases in superstition, as may particularly be observed of gamesters and sailors, who, though of all mankind the least capable of serious reflection, abound most in frivolous and superstitious apprehensions. The gods, says Coriolanus in Dionysius, have an influence in every affair; but above all in war, where the event is so uncertain. All human life, especially before the institution of order and good government, being subject to fortuitous accidents, it is natural that superstition should prevail everywhere in barbarous ages, and put men on the most earnest inquiry concerning those invisible powers, who dispose of their happiness or misery. Ignorant of astronomy and the anatomy of plants and animals, and too little curious to observe the admirable adjustment of final causes, they remain still unacquainted with a first and a Supreme Creator, and with that infinitely Perfect Spirit, who alone, by his almighty will, bestowed order on the whole frame of nature. Such a magnificent idea is too big for their narrow conceptions, which can neither observe the beauty of the work, nor comprehend the grandeur of its author. They suppose their deities, however potent and invisible, to be nothing but a species of human creatures, perhaps raised from among mankind, and retaining all human passions and appetites, together with corporeal limbs and organs. Such limited beings, though masters of human fate, being each of them incapable of extending his influence everywhere, must be vastly multiplied, in order to answer that variety of events which happen over the whole face of nature. Thus every place is stored with a crowd of local deities; and thus polytheism has prevailed, and still prevails, among the greatest part of uninstructed mankind.

2. Rousseau: The Religion of Feeling

Jean-Jacques Rousseau's *Émile* (1762) is beyond doubt the most influential work in the history of modern education. The author describes how a perfect tutor would year by year raise one of his charges in accordance with the dictates of nature. In this section young Émile listens to a virtuous vicar of Savoy expound intimate religious beliefs that are founded upon feelings and the voice of conscience rather than upon rationalistic argument about the existence of God. The translation by William Kenrick appeared in London, 1762-1763 under the title *Emilius and Sophia: or a new system of education.*

I feel that I have a soul, I know it both from thought and sentiment; I know that it exists, without knowing its essence; I cannot reason, therefore, on ideas which I have not. One thing, indeed, I know very well, which is that the identity of my being, can be preserved only by the memory, and that to be in fact the same person, I must remember to have before existed. Now I cannot recollect, after my death, what I was during life; without recollecting also my perceptions and consequently my actions: and I doubt not but this remembrance will one day constitute the happiness of the just and the torments of the wicked. Here below, the violence of our passions absorbs the innate sentiment of right and wrong, and stifles remorse. The mortification and disgrace also, under which virtue labors in the world, prevents our being sensible of its charms. But, when delivered from the delusions of sense, we shall enjoy the contemplation of the Supreme Being, and those eternal truths of which he is the source; when the beauty of the natural order of things, shall strike all the faculties of the soul, and when we shall be employed solely in comparing what we have really done, with what we ought to have done, then will the voice of conscience reassume its tone and strength; then will that pure delight, which arises from a consciousness of virtue, and the bitter regret of having debased ourselves by vice, determine the lot which is severally prepared for us. Ask me not, my good friend, if there may not be some other causes of future happiness and misery. I confess I am ignorant; these, however, which I conceive are sufficient to console me under the inconveniences of this life, and give me hopes of another. I do not pretend to say that the virtuous will receive any peculiar rewards; for what other advantage can a Being, excellent in its own nature expect than to exist in a manner agreeable to the excellence of its constitution? I dare affirm nevertheless that they will be happy; because their Creator, the author of all justice, having given them sensibility cannot have made them to be miserable; and, as they have not abused their liberty on earth, they have not perverted the design of their creation by their own fault: yet, as they have suffered evils in this life, they will certainly be indemnified in another. This opinion is not so much founded on the merits of man, as on the notion of that goodness which appears to me inseparable from the divine nature. I only suppose the order of things strictly maintained, and that the Deity is ever consistent with himself.

It would be to as little purpose to ask me whether the torments of the wicked will be eternal: Of this I am also equally ignorant, and have not the vain curiosity to perplex myself with such useless disquisitions. What is it to me what becomes of the wicked? I interest myself very little in their destiny. I can never believe, however, that they will be condemned to everlasting torments.

If supreme justice avenges itself on the wicked, it avenges itself on them here below. It is you and your errors, ye nations! that are its ministers of vengeance. It employs the evils you bring on each other, to punish the crimes for which you deserve them. It is in the insatiable hearts of mankind, corroding with envy, avarice, and ambition, that their avenging passions punish them for their vices, amidst all the false appearances of prosperity. Where is the necessity of seeking a hell in another life, when it is to be found even in this, in the hearts of the wicked?

Where our momentary necessities or senseless desires have an end, there ought our passions and our vices to end also. Of what perversity can pure spirits be susceptible? As they stand in need of nothing, to what end should they be vicious? If destitute of our grosser senses, all their happiness consists in the contemplation of things, they cannot be desirous of any thing but good; and whoever ceases to be wicked, is it possible he should be eternally miserable? This is what I am inclined to believe on this head, without giving myself the trouble to determine positively concerning the matter.—O righteous and merciful Being! Whatever be thy decrees, I acknowledge their rectitude; if thou punishest the wicked, my weak reason is dumb before thy justice. But, if the remorse of these unfortunate wretches is to have an end, if the same fate is one day to attend us all, my soul exults in thy praise. Is not the wicked man, after all, my brother? How often have I been tempted to resemble him in partaking of his vices. O, may he be delivered from his misery; may he cast off also, that malignity which accompanies it; may he be ever happy as myself; so far from exciting my jealousy, his happiness will only add to mine.

It is thus that contemplating God in his works, and studying him in those attributes which it imports me to know, I learn by degrees to extend that imperfect and confined idea I at first formed of the Supreme Being. But, if this idea becomes thus more grand and noble, it is proportionably less adapted to the weakness of the human understanding. In proportion, as my mind approaches eternal light, its lightness dazzles and confounds me; so that I am forced to give up all those mean and earthly images which assist my imagination. God is no longer a corporeal and preceptible Being; the Supreme Intelligence which governs the world, is no longer the world itself: but in vain I endeavour to raise my thoughts to a conception of his essence. When I reflect that it is he who gives life and activity to that living and active substance, which moves and governs animated bodies; when I am told that my soul is a spiritual Being, and that God also is a spirit, I am incensed at this debasement of the divine essence, as if God and my soul were of the same nature, as if God was not the only absolute, the only truly active Being, perceiving, thinking and willing of himself, from whom his creatures derive thought, activity, will, liberty and existence. We are free only because it is his will that we should be so; his inexplicable substance being, with respect to our souls, such as our souls are in regard to our bodies. I know nothing of his having created matter, bodies, spirits, or the world. The idea of creation confounds me and surpasses my conception, though I believe as much of it as I am able to conceive: but I know that he hath formed the universe, and all that exists in the most consummate order. God is doubtless eternal, but I am incapacitated to conceive an idea of eternity. Why then should I amuse myself with words? All that I conceive is, that he existed before all things, that he exists with them, and will exist after them, if they should ever have an end. That a Being, whose essence is inconceivable, should give existence to other beings, is at best obscure and incomprehensible to our ideas; but that something and nothing should be reciprocally converted into each other, is a palpable contradiction, a most manifest absurdity.

God is intelligent; but in what manner? Man is intelligent by the act of reasoning, but the supreme intelligence lies under no necessity to reason. He requires neither premises, nor consequences; not even the simple form of a proposition: his knowledge is purely intuitive; he beholds equally what is and will be; all truths are to him as one idea, as all places are but one point, and all times one moment. Human power acts by the use of means, the divine power in and of itself. God is powerful because he is willing, his will constituting his power. God is good, nothing is more manifest than this truth; goodness in man, however, consists in a love to his fellow-creatures, and the goodness of God in a love of order: for it is on such order that the connection and preservation of all things depend. Again, God is just; this I am fully convinced of, as it is the natural consequence of his goodness. The injustice of men is their own work, not his; and that moral disorder, which, in the judgment of some philosophers, makes against the system of providence, is in mine the strongest argument for it. Justice in man, indeed, is to render every one his due; but the justice of God requires, at the hands of every one, an account of the talents with which he has entrusted them.

In the discovery, however, by the force of reason, of those divine attributes, of which I have no absolute idea, I only affirm what I do not clearly comprehend, which is in effect to affirm nothing. I may say, it is true that God is this or that; I may be sensible of it, and fully convinced within myself that he is so, I am yet never the better able to conceive how, or in what manner, he so is.

In short, the greater efforts I make to contemplate his infinite essence, the less I am able to conceive it: But I am certain that he is, and that is sufficient; the more he surpasses my conceptions, the more I adore him. I humble myself before him, and say, "Being of beings, I am, because thou art; to meditate continually on thee, is to elevate my thoughts to the fountain of existence. The most meritorious use of my reason is to be annihilated before thee: it is the delight of my soul, to feel my weak faculties overcome by the splendor of thy greatness."

After having thus deduced, from the impressions of perceptible objects, and that innate principle which leads me to judge of natural causes from experience, the most important truth; it remains for me to enquire what maxims I ought to draw from them, for my conduct in life, what rules I ought to prescribe to myself, in order to fulfil my destination on earth, agreeable to the design of him who placed me here. To pursue my own method, I deduce not these rules from the sublime principles of philosophy; but find them written in indelible characters on my heart. I have only to consult myself concerning what I ought to do; all that I feel to be right, is right; whatever I feel to be wrong, is wrong: conscience is the ablest of all casuists, and it is only when we are trafficking with her, that we have recourse to the subtilties of logical ratiocination. The chief of our concerns is that of ourselves; yet how often have we not been told by the monitor within, that to pursue our own interest at the expence of others would be to do wrong! we imagine thus, that we are sometimes obeying the impulse of nature, and we are all the while resisting it: In listening to the voice of our senses, we turn a deaf ear to the dictates of our hearts, the active Being obeys, the passive Being commands. Conscience is the voice of the soul, the passions are the voice of the body. Is it surprizing that these two voices should sometimes contradict each other; or can it be doubted, when they do, which ought to be obeyed? Reason deceives us but too often, and has given us a right to distrust her conclusions; but conscience never deceives us. She is man's truest and safest guide; conscience is in the soul, what instinct is in the body. Whoever puts himself under the conduct of this guide, pursues the direct path of nature, and need not fear to be misled.

3. D'Holbach: The Priestly Religion

Paul Heinrich Dietrich, the Baron d'Holbach, was the Maecenas of the radical wing of the *philosophes*. In his salon they ate, drank, conversed, and blasphemed. With their aid he turned out a steady stream of anti-clerical writings that were often adaptations of works by extremist English deists of an earlier generation. Like his *Hell Destroyed* and *Christianity Unveiled*, Holbach's *Common Sense, or Natural ideas opposed to Supernatural* (1772) was a brief epitome of atheistic arguments; many of the same ideas had already been set forth in the more extensive *System of Nature* (1770). We reproduce the whole of the preface of *Common Sense* in a 1795 translation which appeared both in New York and Philadelphia, proof that these ideas had quickly made their way across the Atlantic.

When we coolly examine the opinions of men, we are surprised to find, that in those, which they regard as the most essential, nothing is more uncommon than the use of common sense; or, in other words, a degree of judgment sufficient to discover the most simple truths, to reject the most striking absurdities, and to be shocked with palpable contradictions. We have an example of it in theology, a science revered in all times and countries, by the greatest number of men; an object they regard as the most important, the most useful, and the most indispensable to the happiness of societies. Indeed, with little examination of the principles, upon which this pretended science is founded, we are forced to acknowledge, that these principles, judged incontestable, are only hazardous suppositions, imagined by ignorance, propagated by enthusiasm or knavery, adopted by timid credulity, preserved by custom, which never reasons, and revered solely because not understood. *Some,* says Monta[i]gne, *make the world think, that they believe what they do not; others, in greater number, make themselves think, that they believe what they do not, not knowing what belief is.*

In a word, whoever will deign to consult common sense upon

religious opinions, and bestow in this inquiry the attention that is commonly given to objects, we presume interesting, will easily perceive, that these opinions have no foundation; that all religion is an edifice in the air; that theology is only the ignorance of natural causes reduced to system; that it is a long tissue of chimeras and contradictions. That it represents, in every country, to the different nations of the earth, only romances void of probability, the hero of which is himself composed of qualities impossible to combine; that his name, exciting in all hearts respect and fear, is only a vague word, which men have continually in their mouths, without being able to affix to it ideas or qualities, which are not contradicted by facts, or evidently inconsistent with one another.

The idea of this being, of whom we have no idea, or rather, the word by which he is designated, would be an indifferent thing, did it not cause innumerable ravages in the world. Prepossessed with the opinion, that this phantom is an interesting reality, men, instead of concluding wisely from its incomprehensibility, that they are not bound to regard it; on the contrary infer, that they cannot sufficiently meditate upon it, that they must contemplate it without ceasing, reason upon it without end, and never lose sight of it. Their invincible ignorance, in this respect, far from discouraging them, irritates their curiosity; instead of putting them upon guard against their imagination, this ignorance renders them decisive, dogmatical, imperious, and even exasperates them against all, who oppose doubts to the reveries, which their brains have begotten.

What perplexity arises, when it is required to solve an insolvable problem! Restless meditations upon an object, impossible to understand, in which, however, he thinks himself much concerned, cannot but put man in a very ill humor, and produce in his head dangerous transports. Let interest, vanity and ambition, co-operate ever so little with these dispositions, and society must necessarily be disturbed. This is the reason that so many nations have often been the theatres of the extravagances of senseless dreamers, who, believing, or publishing their empty speculations as eternal truths, have kindled the enthusiasm of princes and people, and armed them for opinions, which they represented as essential to the glory of the Deity, and the happiness of empires. In all parts of our globe, intoxicated fanatics have been seen cutting each other's throats, lighting funeral piles, committing, without scruple and even as a duty, the greatest crimes, and shedding torrents of blood. For what? To strengthen, support, or propagate the impertinent conjectures of some enthusiasts, or to give validity to the cheats of some impostors, in the name and behalf of a being, who exists only in their imagination, and who has made himself known only by the ravages, disputes, and follies, he has caused upon the earth.

Fierce and uncultivated nations, perpetually at war, have in their origin, under divers names, adored some God, conformable to their ideas; that is to say, cruel, carnivorous, selfish, blood-thirsty. We find, in all religions of the earth, a *God of armies,* a *jealous God,* an *avenging God,* a *destroying God,* a *God,* who is pleased with carnage, and whom his worshippers, as a duty, serve to his taste. Lambs, bulls, children, men, heretics, infidels, kings, whole nations are sacrificed to him. Do not the zealous servants of this so barbarous God, even think it a duty to offer up themselves as a sacrifice to him? We every where see madmen, who, after dismal meditations upon their terrible God, imagine, that to please him, they must do themselves all possible injury, and inflict on themselves, for his honor, invented torments. In short, the gloomy ideas of the divinity, far from consoling men under the evils of life, have every where disquieted and confused their minds, and produced follies destructive to their happiness.

Infested with frightful phantoms, and guided by men, interested in perpetuating its ignorance and fears, how could the human mind have made any considerable progress? Man has been forced to vegetate in his primitive stupidity; nothing has been offered to his mind, but stories of invisible powers, upon whom his happiness was supposed to depend. Occupied solely by his fears, and unintelligible reveries, he has always been at the mercy of his priests, who have reserved to themselves the right of thinking for him, and directing his actions.

Thus man has been, and ever will remain, a child without experience, a slave without courage, a stupid animal, who has feared to reason, and who has never known how to extricate himself from the labyrinth, where his ancestors had strayed. He has believed himself forced to groan under the yoke of his gods, whom he has known only by the fabulous accounts of his ministers, who, after having bound him with the chords of opinion, have remained his masters; or rather have abandoned him, defenceless, to the absolute power of tyrants, no less terrible than the gods, whose representatives they have been upon earth.

Crushed under the double yoke of spiritual and temporal power, it was impossible for the people to know and pursue their happiness. As religion, politics, and morality became sanctuaries, into which the ungodly were not permitted to enter, men had no other morality, than what their legislators and priests brought down from the unknown regions of the Empyrean. The human mind, confused with its theological opinions, forgot itself, doubted its own powers, mistrusted experience, feared truth, disdained its reason, and abandoned her direction, blindly to follow authority. Man was a mere machine in the hands of his tyrants and priests, who alone had the right of directing his actions; always led like a slave, he ever had his vices and character. These are the true causes of the corruption of morals, to which religion ever opposes only ideal barriers, and that without effect. Ignorance and servitude are calculated to make men wicked and unhappy. Knowledge, reason, and liberty can alone reform them, and make them happier; but every thing conspires to blind them, and confirm their errors. Priests cheat them, tyrants corrupt, the better to enslave them. Tyranny ever was, and ever will be, the true cause of the corruption of morals, and the habitual calamities of men; who, almost always fascinated with religious notions, and metaphysical fictions, instead of turning their eyes to the natural and obvious causes of their misery, attribute their vices to the imperfection of their nature, and their unhappiness to the anger of the gods. They offer up to heaven vows, sacrifices, and presents, to obtain the end of their sufferings, which, in reality, are chargeable only to the negligence, ignorance, and perversity of their guides, the folly of their institutions, their silly customs, false opinions, irrational laws, and above all, to the want of knowledge. Let men's minds be filled with true ideas; let their reason be cultivated; let justice govern them; and there will be no need of opposing to the passions, such a feeble barrier, as a fear of gods. Men will be good, when they are well instructed, well governed, and when they are punished or despised for the evil, and justly rewarded for the good, they do to their fellow-creatures.

In vain should we attempt to cure men of their vices, unless we begin by curing them of their prejudices. It is only by shewing them the truth, that they will know their dearest interests, and the motives that ought to incline them to do good. Instructors have long enough fixed men's eyes upon heaven, let them now turn them upon earth. Fatigued with an inconceivable theology, ridiculous fables, impenetrable mysteries, puerile ceremonies, let the human mind apply itself to the study of nature, to intelligible objects, sensible truths, and useful knowledge. Let the vain chimeras of men be removed, and reasonable opinions will soon come of themselves, into those heads, which were thought to be forever destined to error.

Does it not suffice to annihilate or shake religious prejudices, to shew, that what is inconceivable to man, cannot be made for him? Does it then require any thing, but plain, common sense, to perceive, that a being incompatible with the most evident notions; that a cause continually opposed to the effects, which we attribute to it; that a being, of whom we can say nothing, without falling into contradiction; that a being, who, far from explaining the enigmas of the universe, only makes them more inexplicable; that a being, whom for so many ages men have so vainly addressed to obtain their happiness, and the end of their sufferings; does it require, I say, any thing but plain, common sense, to perceive, that the idea of such a being is an idea without model, and that it is evidently only a being of imagination? Is any thing necessary but common sense to perceive, at least, that it is madness and folly to hate and torment one another for unintelligible opinions upon a being of this kind? In short, does not every thing prove, that morality and virtue are totally incompatible with the notions of a God, whom his ministers and interpreters have described in every country, as the most capricious, unjust, and cruel of tyrants, whose pretended will, however, must serve as law and rule to the inhabitants of the earth?

To learn the true principles of morality, men have no need of theology, of revelation, or gods: They have need only of reason. They have only to enter into themselves, to reflect upon their own nature, consult their sensible interests, consider the object of society, and of the individuals, who compose it; and they will easily perceive, that virtue is the interest, and vice the unhappiness of beings of their kind. Let us persuade men to be just, beneficent, moderate, sociable; not because the gods demand it, but because they must please men. Let us advise them to abstain from vice and crimes; not because they will be punished in the other world, but because they will suffer for it in this.—*There are,* says a great man, *means to prevent crimes—these are punishments; there are those to reform manners—these are good examples.*

Truth is simple; error is complex, uncertain in its progress, and full of windings. The voice of nature is intelligible; that of falsehood is ambiguous, enigmatical, mysterious; the way of truth is straight; that of imposture is crooked and dark. Truth, forever necessary to man, must necessarily be felt by all upright minds; the lessons of reason are formed to be followed by all honest men. Men are unhappy only because they are ignorant; they are ignorant only because every thing conspires to prevent their being enlightened; they are so wicked only because their reason is not yet sufficiently unfolded.

By what fatality then, have the first founders of all sects given to their gods the most ferocious characters, at which nature recoils? Can we imagine a conduct more abominable, than that ascribed by Moses to his God, towards the Egyptians, where that assassin proceeds boldly to declare, in the name, and by the order of *his* God, that Egypt shall be afflicted with the greatest calamities, that can happen to man. Of all the different ideas, which they wish to give us of a supreme being, of a God, creator and preserver of men, there are none more horrible, than those of these impostors, who believed themselves inspired by a divine spirit.

Why, O theologians! do you presume to rummage in the impenetrable mysteries of a first being, whom you call inconceivable to the human mind. You are the first blasphemers, in attributing to a being, perfect according to you, so many horrors, committed towards creatures, whom he has made out of nothing. Confess, with us, your ignorance of a creating God; and forbear, in your turn, to meddle with mysteries, which man seems unworthy of knowing.

4. Lessing: A Lesson in Religious Toleration

Gotthold Ephraim Lessing was one of the most versatile figures of the German Enlightenment—dramatist, art critic, philosopher of history, religious and moral teacher. In his play, *Nathan the Wise* (1779), he preached tolerance and respect for all forms of religion by adapting an age-old parable. This scene presents the wise and virtuous Nathan—for whom Lessing's friend the German Jewish philosopher Moses Mendelssohn was the prototype—answering Saladin's insistent question, "Which is the true religion?" This translation by William Jacks appeared in Glasgow, 1894.

NATHAN

In days of yore a man lived in the East,
Who owned a ring of marvellous worth,
Given to him by a hand beloved.
The stone was opal, and shed a hundred lovely rays,
But chiefly it possessed the secret power
To make the owner loved of God and man,
If he but wore it in this faith and confidence;
What wonder then that this man in the East
Ne'er from his finger took the ring,
And so arranged it should forever with his house remain,
Namely, thus: He bequeathed it to
The most belovèd of his sons,
Firmly prescribing that he in turn
Should leave it to the dearest of his sons;
And always thus the dearest, without respect to birth,
Became the head and chieftain of the house
By virtue of the ring alone.
You understand me, Sultan?

SALADIN

> I understand. Proceed.

NATHAN

The ring, descending thus from son to son,
Came to the father of three sons at last,
All three of whom obeyed him equally,
And all of whom he therefore loved alike.
From time to time indeed, now one seemed worthiest of the ring,
And now another, now the third,
Just as it happened one or other with him were alone,
And his o'erflowing heart was not divided with the other two;
And so to each one of the three he gave
The promise—in pious weakness done—
He should possess the wondrous ring.
This then went on long as it could;
But then at last it came to dying,
Which brings the father into sore perplexity.
It pains him much to practise such deceit
Upon two sons who rested so upon his word.
What can be done? In secret
He seeks out a skilful artist,
And from him orders yet two other rings,
Just to the pattern of his own,
And urges him to spare neither pains nor gold,
To make a perfect match.
The artist so succeeded in his task,
That, when he brought the jewels home,
The father even failed to tell which was the pattern ring.
Now, glad and joyous, he calls his sons—
But separately of course—gives each
A special blessing with his ring, and dies.
You hear me, Sultan?

SALADIN

(Who, somewhat moved, turns from him)

> **I hear, I hear;**

But pray get ended with your tale.
You soon will be?

NATHAN

> I'm at the end,

For what still follows is self-understood.
Scarce was the father dead,
When each one with his ring appears
Claiming each the headship of the house.
Inspections, quarrelling, and complaints ensue;
But all in vain, the veritable ring
Was not distinguishable—

> *(After a pause, during which he expects the*
> *Sultan's answer)*

Almost as indistinguishable as to us,
Is now—the true religion.

SALADIN

What? Is that meant as answer to my question?

NATHAN

'Tis meant but to excuse myself, because
I lack the boldness to discriminate between the rings,
Which the father by express intent had made
So that they might not be distinguished.

SALADIN

The rings! Don't play with me.
I thought the faiths which I have named
Were easily distinguishable,
Even to their raiment, even to meat and drink.

NATHAN

But yet not as regards their proofs;
For do not all rest upon history, written or traditional?
And history can also be accepted
Only on faith and trust. Is it not so?

Now, whose faith and confidence do we least misdoubt?
That of our relatives? Of those whose flesh and blood we are,
Of those who from our childhood
Have lavished on us proofs of love,
Who ne'er deceived us, unless 'twere wholesome for us so?
How can I place less faith in my forefathers
Than you in yours? or the reverse?
Can I desire of you to load your ancestors with lies,
So that you contradict not mine? Or the reverse?
And to the Christian the same applies.
Is that not so?

SALADIN

[By the living God, the man is right. I must be dumb.]

NATHAN

Let us return unto our rings.
As said, the sons accused each other,
And each one swore before the judge
He had received his ring directly
From his father's hand—which was quite true—
And that, indeed, after having long his promise held,
To enjoy eventually the ring's prerogative,
Which was no less the truth.
Each one insisted that it was impossible
His father could play false with him,
And ere he could suspect so dear and true a father,
He was compelled, howe'er inclined to think
The best of them, to accuse his brothers
Of this treacherous act, to unmask the traitors,
And avenge himself.

SALADIN

                                    Well, and the judge?
I'm curious to hear what you will give
The judge to say. Go on.

NATHAN

The judge said this: Produce your father here
At once, or I'll dismiss you from this court.
Think you I'm here but to solve riddles?
Or would you wait till the true ring itself will speak?
But stop; I've just been told that the right ring,
Contains the wondrous gift to make its wearer loved,
Agreeable alike to God and man.
That must decide, for the false rings will not have this power.
Now which one do the other two love most?
Come, speak out; you're silent?
Do the rings work only backwards and not outwardly?
Does each one love himself the best?
Then you're all three deceived deceivers;
None of your rings are genuine.
The genuine ring is no doubt lost.
To hide the loss and to supply its place
The father ordered other three.

SALADIN

Splendid, splendid!

NATHAN

The judge went further on to say:
If you will have my judgment, not my advice,
Then go. But my advice is this:
You take the matter as it stands.
If each one had his ring straight from his father,
So let each believe *his* ring the true one.
'Tis possible your father would no longer tolerate
The tyranny of this one ring in his family,
And surely loved you all—and all alike,
And that he would not two oppress
By favouring the third.
Now then, let each one emulate in affection
Untouched by prejudice. Let each one strive

To gain the prize of proving by results
The virtue of his ring, and aid its power
With gentleness and heartiest friendliness,
With benevolence and true devotedness to God;
And if the virtue of the ring will then
Have proved itself among your children's children.
I summon them to appear again
Before this judgment seat,
After a thousand thousand years.
Here then will sit a judge more wise than I,
Who will pronounce. Go you.
So said the modest judge.

SALADIN

God, oh God!

NATHAN

Saladin, if now you feel yourself to be
That promised sage—

SALADIN

(*Who rushes to him and seizes his hand, which to the end he
does not let go*)

I dust? I nothing? Oh God!

NATHAN

What ails thee, Sultan?

SALADIN

Nathan, dear Nathan, your judge's thousand
Thousand years have not yet fled,
His judgment seat's not become mine.
Go, go; but be my friend.

Part Three
HUMAN NATURE

1. Hutcheson: Concerning the Moral Sense

Eighteenth-century writers often debated over whether men were driven only by self-interest or whether there was not an inborn sympathy, fellow-feeling or benevolence toward other human beings. The Scottish philosophers tended to belong to this latter group, the "moral sense" school, of whom Francis Hutcheson is a representative figure. The excerpt is from the first volume of *A System of Moral Philosophy* (London, 1755).

There is therefore, as each one by close attention and reflection may convince himself, a natural and immediate determination to approve certain affections, and actions consequent upon them; or a natural sense of immediate excellence in them, not referred to any other quality perceivable by our other senses or by reasoning. When we call this determination a *sense* or *instinct,* we are not supposing it of that low kind dependent on bodily organs, such as even the brutes have. It may be a constant setled determination in the soul itself, as much as our powers of judging and reasoning. And 'tis pretty plain that *reason* is only a subservient power to our ultimate determinations either of perception or will. The ultimate end is setled by some sense, and some determination of will: by some sense we enjoy happiness, and self-love determines to it without reasoning. Reason can only direct to the means; or compare two ends previously constituted by some other immediate powers.

In other animal-kinds each one has instincts toward its proper action, and has the highest enjoyment in following them, even with toil and some pain. Can we suppose mankind void of such principles? as brutes seem not to reflect on their own temper and actions, or that of others, they may feel no more than present delight in following their impulses. But in men, who can make their own tempers and conduct the objects of reflection, the analogy of nature would make one expect a sense, a relish about them, as well as about other objects. To each of our powers we seem to have a corresponding taste or sense, recommending the proper use of it to the agent, and making him relish or value the like exercise of it by another. This we see as to the powers of voice, of imitation, designing, or machinery, motion, reasoning; there is a sense discerning and recommending the proper exercise of them. It would be anomalous in our structure if we had no relish or taste for powers and actions of yet greater importance; if a species of which each one is naturally capable of very contrary affections toward its fellows, and of consequent actions, each one also requiring a constant intercourse of actions with them, and dependant on them for his subsistence, had not an immediate relish for such affections and actions as the interest of the system requires. Shall an immediate sense recommend the proper use of the inferior powers, and yet shall we allow no natural relish for that of the superior?

As some others of our immediate perceptive powers are capable of culture and improvement, so is this moral sense, without presupposing any reference to a superior power of reason to which their perceptions are to be referred. We once had pleasure in the simple artless tunes of the vulgar. We indulge ourselves in musick; we meet with finer and more complex compositions. In these we find a pleasure much higher, and begin to despise what formerly pleased us. A judge, from the motions of pity, gets many criminals acquitted: we approve this sweet tenderness of heart. But we find that violence and outrages abound; the sober, just, and industrious are plagued, and have no security. A more extensive view of a publick interest shews some sorts of pity to occasion more extensive misery, than arises from a strict execution of justice. Pity of itself never appears deformed; but a more extensive affection, a love to society, a zeal to promote general happiness, is a more lovely principle, and the want of this renders a character deformed. This only shews, what we shall presently confirm, that among the several affections approved there are many degrees: some much more lovely than others. 'Tis thus alone we correct any apparent disorders in this *moral faculty*, even as we correct our reason itself. As we improve and correct a low taste for harmony by enuring the ear to finer compositions; a low taste for beauty, by presenting the finer works, which yield an higher pleasure; so we improve our *moral taste* by presenting larger systems to our mind, and more extensive affections toward them; and thus finer objects are exhibited to the moral faculty, which it will approve, even when these affections oppose the effect of some narrower affections, which considered by themselves would be truly lovely. No need here of reference to an higher power of perception, or to reason.

Is not our reason itself also often wrong, when we rashly conclude from imperfect or partial evidence? must there be an higher power too to correct our reason? no; presenting more fully all the evidence on both sides, by serious attention, or the best exercise of the reasoning power, corrects the hasty judgment. Just so in the moral perceptions.

This moral sense from its very nature appears to be designed for regulating and controlling all our powers. This dignity and commanding nature we are immediately conscious of, as we are conscious of the power itself. Nor can such matters of immediate feeling be otherways proved but by appeals to our hearts. It does not estimate the good it recommends as merely differing in degree, tho' of the same kind with other advantages recommended by other senses, so as to allow us to practise smaller moral evils acknowledged to remain such, in order to obtain some great advantages of other sorts; or to omit what we judge in the present case to be our duty or morally good, that we may decline great evils of another sort. But as we immediately perceive the difference in kind, and that the dignity of enjoyment from fine poetry, painting, or from knowledge is superior to the pleasures of the palate, were they never so delicate; so we immediately discern moral good to be superior in kind and dignity to all others which are perceived by the other perceptive powers.

In all other grateful perceptions, the less we shall relish our taste, the greater sacrifice we have made of inferior enjoyments to the superior; and our sense of the superior, after the first flutter of joy in our success is over, is not a whit increased by any sacrifice we have made to it: nay in the judgment of spectators, the superior enjoyment, or our state at least, is generally counted the worse on this account, and our conduct the less relished. Thus in sacrificing ease, or health, or pleasure, to wealth, power, or even to the ingenious arts; their pleasures gain no dignity by that means; and the conduct is not more alluring to others. But in moral good, the greater the necessary sacrifice was which was made to it, the moral excellence increases the more, and is the more approved by the agent, more admired by spectators, and the more they are roused to imitation. By this sense the heart can not only approve itself in sacrificing every other gratification to moral goodness, but have the highest self-enjoyment, and approbation of its own disposition in doing so: which plainly shews this moral sense to be naturally destined to command all the other powers.

To acknowledge the several generous ultimate affections of a limited kind to be natural, and yet maintain that we have no general controlling principle but self-love, which indulges or checks the generous affections as they conduce to, or oppose, our own noblest interest; sometimes allowing these kind affections their full exercise, because of that high enjoyment we expect to ourselves in gratifying them; at other times checking them, when their gratification does not over-ballance the loss we may sustain by it; is a scheme which brings indeed all the powers of the mind into one direction by means of the reference made of them all to the calm desire of our own happiness, in our previous deliberations about our conduct: and it may be justly alledged that the Author of Nature has made a connexion in the event at last between our gratifying our generous affections, and our own highest interest. But the feelings of our heart, reasons, and history, revolt against this account: which seems however to have been maintained by excellent authors and strenuous defenders of the cause of virtue.

This connexion of our own highest interests with the gratifying our generous affections, in many cases is imperceptible to the mind; and the kind heart acts from its generous impulse, not thinking of its own interest. Nay all its own interests have sometimes appeared to it as opposite to, and inconsistent with the generous part, in which it persisted. Now were there no other calm original determination of soul but that toward one's own interest, that man must be approved intirely who steadily pursues his own happiness, in opposition to all kind affections and all publick interest. That which is the sole calm determination, must justify every action in consequence of it, however opposite to particular kind affections. If it be said "that 'tis a mistake to imagine our interest opposite to them while there is a good providence:" grant it to be a mistake; this is only a defect of reasoning; but that disposition of mind must upon this scheme be approved which coolly sacrifices the interest of the universe to its own interest. This is plainly contrary to the feelings of our hearts.

Can that be deemed the sole ultimate determination, the sole ultimate end, which the mind in the exercise of its noblest powers can calmly resolve, with inward approbation, deliberately to counteract? are there not instances of men who have voluntarily sacrificed their lives, without thinking of any other state of existence, for the sake of their friends or their country? does not every heart approve this temper and conduct, and admire it the more, the less presumption there is of the love of glory and posthumous fame, or of any sublimer private interest mixing itself with the generous affection? does not the admiration rise higher, the more deliberately such resolutions are formed and executed? all this is unquestionably true, and yet would be absurd and impossible if self-interest of any kind is the sole ultimate termination of all calm desire. There is therefore another ultimate determination which our souls are capable of, destined to be also an original spring of the calmest and most deliberate purposes of action; a desire of communicating happiness, an ultimate good-will, not referred to any private interest, and often operating without such reference.

In those cases where some inconsistency appears between these two determinations, the moral faculty at once points out and recommends the glorious, the amiable part; not by suggesting prospects of future interests of a sublime sort by pleasures of self-approbation, or of praise. It recommends the generous part by an immediate undefinable perception; it approves the kind ardour of the heart in the sacrificing even of life itself, and that even in those who have no hopes of surviving, or no attention to a future life in another world. And thus, where the moral sense is in its full vigour, it makes the generous determination to publick happiness the supreme one in the soul, with that commanding power which it is naturally destined to exercise.

It must be obvious we are not speaking here of the ordinary condition of mankind, as if these calm determinations were generally exercised, and habitually controlled the particular passions; but of the condition our nature can be raised to by due culture; and of the principles which may and ought to operate, when by attention we present to our minds the objects or representations fit to excite them. Doubtless some good men have exercised in life only the particular kind affections, and found a constant approbation of them, without either the most extensive views of the whole system, or the most universal benevolence. Scarce any of the vicious have ever considered wherein it is that their highest private happiness consists, and in consequence of it exerted the calm rational self-love; but merely follow inconsiderately the selfish appetites and affections. Much less have all good men made actual references of all private or generous affections to the extensive benevolence, tho' the mind can make them; or bad men made references of all their affections to calm self-love.

But as the selfish principles are very strong, and by custom, by early and frequent indulgences, and other causes, are raised in the greatest part of men above their due proportion, while the generous principles are little cultivated, and the moral sense often asleep; our powers of reasoning and comparing the several enjoyments which our nature is capable of, that we may discover which of them are of greatest consequence to our happiness; our capacity, by reasoning, of arriving to the knowledge of a *Governing Mind* presiding in this world, and of a moral administration, are of the highest consequence and necessity to preserve our affections in a just order, and to corroborate our *moral faculty:* as by such reasoning and reflection we may discover a perfect consistency of all the generous motions of the soul with private interest, and find out a certain tenor of life and action the most effectually subservient to both these determinations.

2. Helvétius: Moral Sense Denied

Claude Adrien Helvétius presents an argument against both the moral sense school, represented by Hutcheson, and Jean-Jacques Rousseau's belief in the natural goodness of man. He insists that man in the cradle is neither good nor evil. Helvétius is really an adherent of the "clean slate" doctrine in John Locke's sense: all of man's capacities and his principles of morality are exclusively the result of training and experience, and if an appropriate system of education were devised, men, motivated by self-interest alone, could be conditioned to will the good of society. *A Treatise on Man; his intellectual faculties and his education* first appeared in French in 1773; we use the translation by W. Hooper (London, 1777).

Of the Goodness of Man in the Cradle

I love you, O my fellow citizens! and my chief desire is to be useful to you. I doubtless desire your approbation; but shall I owe your esteem and applause to a lie? A thousand others will deceive you; I shall not be their accomplice. Some will say you are good, and flatter the desire you have to think yourselves so: believe them not. Others will say you are wicked, and in like manner will say false. You are neither the one nor the other.

No individual is born good or bad. Men are the one or the other, according as a similar or opposite interest unites or divides them. Philosophers suppose men to be born in a state of war. A common desire to possess the same things arms them from the cradle, say they, against each other.

The state of war, without doubt, closely follows the instant of their birth. The peace between them is of short duration. They are not however both enemies. Goodness or badness is an incident to them; it is the consequence of their good or bad laws. What we call in man his goodness or moral sense, is his benevolence to others;

and that benevolence is always proportionate to the utility they are of to him. I prefer my countrymen to strangers, and my friends to my countrymen. The prosperity of my friend is reflected on me. If he become more rich and powerful, I participate in his riches and power. Benevolence to others is therefore the effect of love for ourselves. Now if self-love . . . be the necessary effect of the faculty of sensation our love for others, whatever the Shaftesburyans may say, is in like manner the effect of the same faculty.

What in fact is that original goodness or moral sense, so much boasted of by the English? What clear idea can we form of such a sense, and on what fact do we found its existence? On the goodness of men? But there are also, persons who are envious and liars, *omnis homo mendax*. Will they say in consequence, that those men have in them an immoral sense of envy, and a lying sense. Nothing is more absurd than this theological philosophy of Shaft[e]sbury; and yet the greatest part of the English are as fond of it as the French were formerly of their music. It is not the same with other nations. No stranger can understand the one or bear the other. It is a web on the eye of the English. It must be taken away before they can see clearly.

According to their philosophy, the man indifferent and seated at his ease, desires the happiness of others: but as being indifferent, he does not, and cannot desire any thing. The states of desire and indifference are contradictory. Perhaps the state of perfect indifference is even impossible. Experience teaches us that man is born neither good nor bad: that his happiness is not necessarily connected with the misery of others: that on the contrary, from a good education, the idea of my own happiness will be always more or less closely connected in my memory with that of my fellow-citizens; and that the desire of the one will produce in me the desire of the other: whence it follows, that the love of his neighbour is in every individual the effect of the love of himself. The most clamorous declaimers for original goodness have not moreover been always the greatest benefactors to humanity.

When the welfare of England was at stake, the idle Shaftesbury, that ardent apostle of the beauty of morality, would not, we are told, even go to the parliament-house to save it. It was not the sense of the beauty of morality, but the love of glory and of their country that formed Horatius Cocles, Brutus, and Scævola. The English philosophers will in vain tell me that beauty of morality is a sense that is developed with the human fœtus, and in a certain time renders man compassionate to the misfortune of his brethren. I can form an idea of my five senses, and of the organs by which they are produced; but I confess I have no more idea of a moral sense, than of a moral castle and elephant.

How long will men continue to use words that are void of meaning, and that not conveying any clear and determinate idea, ought to be for ever banished to the schools of theology. Do they mean by this moral sense the sentiment of compassion felt at the sight of an unhappy object? But to compassionate another man's miseries, we must first know what he suffers, and for that purpose must have felt pain. A compassion on report supposes also a knowledge of misery. Which are the evils moreover that in general we are most sensible of? Those which we suffer with the most impatience, and the remembrance of which is consequently the most habitually present to us. Compassion therefore is not an innate sentiment.

What do I feel at the presence of an unhappy person? A strong emotion. What produces it? The remembrance of pains to which men are subject, and to which I myself am exposed: such an idea troubles me, makes me uneasy, and as long as the unfortunate person is present I am afflicted. When I have assisted him, and see him no more, a calm takes place insensibly in my mind; for in proportion as he is distant from me, the remembrance of the miseries that his presence recalled, insensibly vanishes: when therefore I was afflicted at his presence, it was for myself I was afflicted. Which in fact are the evils I commiserate most. They are, as I have already said, not only those I have felt, but those I may still feel: those evils being most present to my memory, strike me most forcibly. My affliction for the miseries of an unhappy person, is always in proportion to the fear I have of being afflicted with the same miseries. I would, if it were possible, destroy in him the very root of his misfortune, and thereby free myself at the same time from the fear of suffering in the same manner. The love of others is therefore never any thing else in man than an effect of the love of himself, and consequently of his corporeal sensibility. In vain does M. Rousseau repeat incessantly *that all men are good, and all the first movements of nature right.* The necessity of laws proves the contrary. What does this necessity imply? That the different interests of men render them good or bad; and that the only method to form virtuous citizens, is to unite the interest of the individual with that of the public.

At the same time, what man is less convinced than M. Rousseau of the original goodness of characters. He says, "Every man who has not known pain, is ignorant of the tenderness of humanity, or the sweetness of commiseration: his heart is not affected by any thing; he is not sociable, but a monster among his fellow-creatures." He adds, "Nothing, in my opinion, is more true and beautiful than this maxim; *we lament in others those evils only from which we are not exempt:* it is for this reason, (he adds,) that the prince is without pity for his subject, the rich obdurate toward the poor, and the nobleman toward the plebeian."

After these maxims, how maintain the original goodness of man, and pretend that *all characters are good?*

A proof that humanity is nothing more in man than the effect of the misfortunes he has known either by himself or by others is, that of all the ways to render him humane and compassionate, the most efficacious is to habituate him from his most tender age to put himself in the place of the miserable. Some have in consequence treated compassion as a weakness: let them call it so if they please; this weakness will always be in my eyes the first of virtues, because it always contributes the most to the happiness of humanity.

I have proved that compassion is not either a moral sense, or an innate sentiment, but the pure effect of self-love. What follows? That it is this same love, differently modified, according to the different education we receive, and the circumstances, and situations in which chance has placed us, which renders us humane or obdurate: that man is not born compassionate, but that all may and will become so when the laws, the form of government, and their education lead them to it.

O! you, to whom heaven has intrusted the legislative power, let your administration be gentle, your laws sagacious, and you will have subjects humane, valiant, and virtuous! But if you alter either those laws, or that wise administration, those virtuous citizens will expire without posterity, and you will be surrounded by wicked men only; for the laws will make them such. Man, by nature indifferent to evil, will not give himself up to it without a motive: the happy man is humane; he is the couching lion.

Unhappy is the prince who confides in the original goodness of characters; M. Rousseau supposes its existence; experience denies it: whoever consults that, will learn that the child kills flies, beats his dog, and strangles his sparrow; that the child, born without humanity, has all the vices of the man.

The man in power is often unjust; the sturdy child is the same: when he is not restrained by the presence of his master, he appropriates by force, like the man in power, the sweetmeat or play-thing of his companion. He does that for a coral or a doll which he would do at a mature age for a title or a scepter. The uniformity in the manner of acting at those two ages made M. de la Mothe say, *It is because the child is already a man, that the man is still a child.*

The original goodness of characters cannot be maintained by any argument. I will even add, that in man, goodness and humanity cannot be the work of nature, but of education only.

No Two Persons Receive the Same Education

I still learn; my instruction is not yet finished: when will it be? When I shall be no longer sensible; at my death. The course of my life is properly nothing more than a long course of education.

What is necessary in order that two individuals should receive precisely the same education? That they should be in precisely the same positions and the same circumstances. Now such an hypothesis is impossible: it is therefore evident, that no two persons can receive the same instructions.

But why put off the term of our education to the utmost period of life? Why not confine it to the time expressly set apart for instruction, that is, to the period of infancy and adolescence?

I am content to confine it to that period; and I will prove in like manner, that it is impossible for two men to acquire precisely the same ideas.

Of the Moment at Which Education Begins

It is at the very instant a child receives motion and life that it receives its first instruction: it is sometimes even in the womb where it is conceived, that it learns to distinguish between sickness and health. The mother however delivered, the child struggles and cries; hunger gripes it, it feels a want, and that want opens its lips, makes it seize, and greedily suck the nourishing breast. When some months have passed, its sight is distinct, its organs are fortified, it becomes by degrees susceptible of all impressions; then the senses of seeing, hearing, tasting, touching, smelling, in a word, all the inlets to the mind are set open; then all the objects of nature rush thither in crowds, and engrave an infinity of ideas in the memory. In these first moments what can be true instructors of infancy? The various sensations it feels: these are so many instructions it receives.

If two children have the same preceptor, if they are taught to distinguish their letters, to read and repeat their catechism, &c. they are supposed to receive the same education. The philosopher judges otherwise: according to him, the true preceptors of a child are the objects that surround him; these are the instructors to whom he owes almost all his ideas.

Of the Instructors of Childhood

A short history of the infancy of man will bring us acquainted with them. He no sooner sees the light than a thousand sounds strike his ears; he hears nothing but a confused noise; a thousand bodies offer themselves to his sight, but present nothing but objects imperfectly defined. It is by insensible degrees that an infant learns to hear and see, to perceive and rectify the errors of one sense by another.

Being constantly struck by the same sensations in the presence of the same objects, he thereby acquires a more complete remembrance of them, in proportion as the same action of the objects is repeated on him; and this action of them we should regard as the most considerable part of his education.

The child in the mean time grows; he walks and walks alone; numberless falls then teach him to preserve the equilibrium of his body, and to stand firmly on his legs; the more painful the falls, the more instructive they prove, and the more adroitly, attentively, and cautiously he walks.

The child grows strong; he runs, he is already able to leap the little canals that traverse and water the garden. It is then that by repeated trials and falls he learns to proportion his leaps to the width of the canals.

He sees a stone fall into the water and sink to the bottom, while a piece of wood floats on the surface: from this instance he acquires the first idea of gravity.

If he take the stone and the wood out of the water, and by chance they both fall on his feet, the unequal degree of pain occasioned by their fall, engraves more strongly on his memory the idea of their unequal weight and hardness.

If he chance to throw the same stone against one of the flower-pots placed on the borders of a canal, he will then learn that some bodies are broken by a blow that others resist.

There is therefore no man of discernment who must not see in all objects, so many tutors charged with the education of our infancy.

But are not these instructors the same for all? No. The chance is not precisely the same for any two persons; but suppose it were, and that two children owed their dexterity in walking, running, and leaping to their falls; I say, that as it is impossible they should both have precisely the same number of falls, and equally painful, chance cannot furnish them both with the same instructions.

Place two children on a plain, in a wood, a theatre, an assembly, or a shop. They will not, by their natural position, be struck precisely in the same manner, nor consequently affected with the same sensations. What different subjects moreover are by daily occurrences incessantly offered to the view of these two children.

Two brothers travel with their parents, and to arrive at their native place they must traverse long chains of mountains. The eldest follows his father by the short and rugged road. What does he see? Nature in all the forms of horror; mountains of ice that hide their heads among the clouds, massy rocks that hang over the traveller's head, fathomless caverns, and ridges of arid hills, from which torrents rush with a tremendous roar. The younger follows his mother through the most frequented roads, where nature appears in all her pleasing forms. What objects does he behold? Every where hills planted with vines and fruitful trees, and vallies where the wandering streams divide the meadows, peopled by the browzing herds.

These two brothers have, in the same journey, seen very different prospects, and received very different impressions. Now a thousand incidents of the same nature may produce the same effects. Our life it nothing more, so to say, than a long chain of similar incidents; let men never flatter themselves, therefore, with being able to give two children precisely the same education.

What influence moreover may a difference of instruction, occasioned by a trifling difference in surrounding objects, have on the mind? Who does not know that a small number of dissimilar ideas, combined with those which two men already have in common, can produce a total difference in their manner of seeing and judging?

3. La Mettrie: The System of Materialism

Man a Machine. Wherein the several systems of philosophers, in respect to the soul of man are examined; . . . and a full detail is given of the several springs which move the human machine appeared in an English translation disguised as the work of the Marquis d'Argens. The real author was a notorious doctor, Julien Offray de la Mettrie, who had to flee France and seek refuge at the court of Frederick II of Prussia because of his anti-religious beliefs. This little work, which had first been published in French (Leyden, 1748), became the manifesto of the radical materialists. La Mettrie died, it seems, from eating a spoiled meatpie—appropriate punishment for him, the orthodox believed. We have drawn from the opening pages of the 1750 edition.

'Tis not sufficient for a philosopher to study nature and truth; he ought to have courage to speak it in favour of the few that are willing and able to think; for as to the rest, who are voluntary slaves to prejudices, they are no more capable to come at the truth, than frogs to fly.

The systems of philosophers in respect to the soul of man are reducible to two. The first and most ancient is the system of materialism; the second that of spiritualism.

Experiments and observation alone ought to guide us here. These we find in abundance in the writings of such physicians as were philosophers and not in those philosophers who were unacquainted with physic. The former have explored and unravelled the labyrinth of Man. They alone have discovered to us those hidden springs concealed under a cover, which hides from us so many wonders. They alone in a philosophical contemplation of the soul, have a thousand times surprized it in its misery and grandeur; without despising it in one of these conditions, or idolizing it in the other. Once more, I

84

will be bold to say, these are the only authors that have a right to speak on this subject. What would other lame philosophers say, and above all, the divines? Is it not ridiculous to hear them determine without modesty on a subject they have never been qualified to examine thoroughly? a subject from which they have been always diverted by dark idle studies, that have tinctured them with a thousand gross, childish prejudices, and to say all in one word, have plunged them over head and ears in fanaticism, which adds still to their ignorance in the mechanism of bodies.

But tho' we have chosen the best guides, yet we shall find many thorns, and obstacles in our way.

Man is a machine so compound, that it is impossible to form at first a clear idea thereof, and consequently to define it. This is the reason, that all the enquiries the philosophers have made *a priori,* that is, by endeavouring to raise themselves on the wings of the understanding, have proved ineffectual. Thus it is only *a posteriori,* or as it were by disentangling the soul from the organs of the body, that we can, I do not say, discover with evidence the nature of man, but obtain the greatest degree of probability the subject will admit of.

Let us then follow the direction of experience, and not trouble our heads with the vain history of the opinions of philosophers. To be blind, and to think we can do without this guide, is the very height of infatuation. Very justly has it been observed by a modern writer, that nothing but vanity can hinder us from drawing from second causes, what we pretend to infer from the first. We may, and even ought to admire all these subtil geniuses in their most useless labours; I mean the *Descarteses,* the *Mallebranches,* the *Leibnitzes,* &c. but I would fain know, what benefit mankind have reaped from their profound meditations, and from all their works? Let us then see, not what others have thought, but what we ought to think ourselves for the tranquility of our own lives.

As many different constitutions as there are amongst men, so many different minds, characters, and manners. Even *Galen* knew this truth, which *Descartes,* and not *Hypocrates,* as the author of the history of the soul says, has carried so far, as to say, that physic alone could change the minds and manners together with the body. It is true, that melancholy, bile, phlegm, blood, &c. according to the nature, quantity, and different mixture of these humours, not only produce differences in different men, but also render every individual different from what he was, before particular changes were induced in his fluids.

In diseases the soul is sometimes as it were eclipsed, and shews no sign of existence; sometimes one would say it was doubled, so far does passion transport it; sometimes its weakness vanishes, and a fool by the recovery of health, becomes a man of sense. Sometimes the noblest genius in the world sinks into stupidity, and never after recovers. Farewell, then to all those noble acquisitions of learning obtained with so much labour!

Here you may see a paralytic, who asks whether his leg be in bed; there a soldier who believes he still has the arm the surgeon has cut off. The memory of his former sensations, and of the part to which his soul referred them, causes his delusion and species of phrenzy. It suffices to speak to him of the amputated member, to make him recollect and renew, as it were, all its former sensations; which is done with a kind of displeasure of the imagination impossible to be expressed.

One man shall cry like a child at the approaches of death, which another perhaps will laugh at. What was it that could change the intrepidity of *Caius Julius, Seneca,* and *Petronius* into pusillanimity and cowardice? An obstruction in the spleen, the liver, or some disorder in the *vena porta.* Why? Because the imagination is disorder'd at the same time, as the entrails, and hence arise all the different surprizing phaenomena of the hysteric, and hypochondriac affections.

What shall I say of those who believe they are transformed into wolves, cocks, pipkins, or believe that the dead suck, and live upon their blood? Or why should I take notice of those who think they see their noses, or some other member chang'd into glass, and who must be advised to lye on straw for fear of breaking them; to the end that they may find again the use of those parts, and their true flesh, when upon setting fire to the straw, they are afraid of being consumed, a fear which has sometimes cured a palsy? I ought to pass lightly over things that are well known by every body.

Nor shall I dwell upon the effects of sleep. Behold that wearied soldier! he snores in a trench, within the noise of a hundred cannon.

His soul perceives nothing, his sleep is a perfect apoplexy. A bomb is ready to dash him in pieces; perhaps he will less feel this blow, than an insect that lies under his body.

On another side, a man, whom jealousy, hatred, avarice, or ambition devour, is incapable of finding the least repose. The stillest place, the most cooling and refreshing liquors, all become a subject of uneasiness to him, who has not freed his heart from the turbulency of the passions.

The body and soul seem to fall asleep together. In proportion as the motion of the blood grows calm, a soft soothing sense of peace and tranquility spreads itself over the whole machine; the soul finds itself sweetly weighed down with slumber, and sinks with the fibres of the brain: it becomes thus paralitic as it were, by degrees, together with all the muscles of the body. The latter are no longer able to support the head; the head itself can no longer bear the weight of thought; the soul is during sleep, as if it had no existence.

If the circulation goes on with too great rapidity; the soul cannot sleep. If the soul be thrown into too great an agitation, the blood loses its calm, and rushes thro' the veins with a noise that sometimes may be distinctly heard: such are the two reciprocal causes of insomny. A frightful dream makes the heart beat double, and tears us from the sweet necessity of rest, as effectually as a lively pain, or pressing want. In a word, as the sole cessation of the functions of the soul produces sleep, man is subject even during some waking moments (when in reality the soul is no more than half awake) to certain sorts of revery or slumbers of the soul, which are very frequent, and sufficiently prove that the soul does not wait for the body to fall asleep. For if it does not entirely sleep, how little does it want of it? Since it is impossible for her to recollect one object, to which she gave attention, amidst that innumerable crowd of confused ideas, which as so many vanishing clouds had filled up, if I may so say, the atmosphere of the brain.

Opium has too great a relation with sleep, not to give it a place here. This drug intoxicates as well as wine, coffee, &c. every one according to it's nature, and the quantity of the dose. It renders man happy in a state, which one would think to be the grave of all thoughts, as it is the image of death. What a pleasing lethargy! the soul would never be willing to quit it: she was torn as it were to pieces with the sharpest pains; but she has now no other sensation, than of the pleasure of suffering no longer, and of enjoying a charming tranquillity. Opium seems even to change the will; it forces the soul that would fain wake and divert herself, to lie down with the body against her inclination. I wave mentioning here the history of poisons.

'Tis by lashing, as it were, the imagination, that coffee, that antidote of wine, dissipates our head-achs, and chagrins, without making us suffer, as the other liquor often does, the next day.

Let us consider the soul in its other wants. The human body is a machine that winds up its own springs: it is a living image of the perpetual motion. Food nourishes what a fever heats and excites. Without proper food the soul languishes, raves, and dies with faintness. It is like a taper, which revives in the moment it is going to be extinguished. Give but good nourishment to the body, pour into its tubes vigorous juices and strong liquors; then the soul, generous as these, arms itself with courage; and a soldier, whom water would have made run away, becoming undaunted, meets death with alacrity amidst the rattle of drums. Thus it is that hot water agitates the blood, which cold had calmed.

What a vast power there is in a repast! Joy revives in a disconsolate heart; it is transfused into the souls of all the guests, who express it by amiable conversation, or music. The hypochondriac mortal is overpowered with it; and the lumpish pedant is unfit for the entertainment.

Raw meat gives a fierceness to animals; and man would also become fierce by the same nourishment. This is so true, that the *English*, who eat not their meat so well roasted or boiled as we, but red and bloody, seem to partake of this fierceness more or less, which arises in part from such food, and from other causes, which nothing but education can render ineffectual. This fierceness produces in the soul pride, hatred, contempt of other nations, indocility, and other bad qualities that deprave man's character, just as gross phlegmatic meat causes a heavy, cloudy spirit, whose favourite attributes are idleness and indolence.

Mr. *Pope* knew perfectly well the power of gluttony, when he said

> Catius *is ever moral, ever grave,*
> *Thinks who endures a knave, is next a knave:*
> *Save just at dinner—then prefers no doubt,*
> *A rogue with ven'son, to a saint without.*

And a little higher the same poet says,

> *See the same man, in vigour, in the gout,*
> *Alone in company, in place or out;*
> *Early at business, and at hazard late,*
> *Mad at a fox-chase, wise at a debate:*
> *Drunk at a borough, civil at a ball,*
> *Friendly at* Hackney, *faithless at* Whitehall.

There was, in *Switzerland,* a magistrate called Monsieur *Steiguer,* of *Wittighosen:* this gentleman was, when fasting, the most upright and merciful judge; but woe to the wretch who came before him when he had made a hearty dinner! he was then disposed to hang every body, the innocent as well as the guilty.

We think not, nay, we are not honest men, but as we are chearful, or brave; all depends on the manner of winding up our machine. A person would be tempted to think, at certain times, that the soul is lodged in the stomach, and that Van Helmont in placing it in the pylorus, is not deceived but by taking a part for the whole.

To what rage and extravagance cannot hunger drive us? No longer is there any respect shewn to the bowels, to which we owe, or to which we have given life. They are torn and devoured in a detestable feast; and in the madness that seizeth us, the weakest are always sure to fall a prey to the strongest.

Pregnancy, that mimic of the green-sickness, is not contented oftentimes with the depraved longings of the latter disorder; it has sometimes driven a frantic soul into the greatest extravagances; the effects of a sudden madness, which stifles the very sentiments of nature. 'Tis thus the brain, that matrix, if I may use the expression, of the soul, is perverted after its manner, together with that of the body.

Strange is that other kind of madness which is sometimes observable among these men and women, who are forc'd to continency and bless'd with good health. 'Tis not enough for that bashful modest maid to have lost all honour and shame; she makes no more of incest, than a wanton wife does of adultery. If her necessities do not find a quick remedy, they will not be confin'd to symptoms of an uterine affection, of madness, &c. the wretch will die of a disease, for the cure of which the world is stocked with physicians.

We need only have eyes to see the necessary influence which age has over reason. The soul follows the progress of the body, as well as of education. In the fair sex, the soul adapts itself to the delicacy of constitution: thence flow that tenderness, that affection, those lively sentiments founded rather upon passion than reason; and in fine, those prejudices and superstitions whose impression is so hard to be effaced. Man, on the contrary, whose brain and nerves participate of the firmness of all the solids, has his mind, as well as the features of his face, more nervous. Education, which women are deprived of by custom, adds still new degrees of strength to his soul. With such succours, both of nature and art, how should he not be more grateful, more generous, more constant in friendship, more firm in adversity, &c. But according to the opinion of the author of the letters on physiognomy, the sex, which is favoured with the graces of mind and body, together with almost all the tenderest and most delicate sentiments of the heart, ought not to envy man this double strength of body and mind, which seem to have been bestowed upon him for no other end but in order to render him more sensible of the attractives of beauty, and more subservient to the pleasures of that amiable part of the creation.

4. Diderot: The Alienated Man

Rameau's Nephew by Denis Diderot was not published during his life-time. This imaginary dialogue in a Paris café between the author playing the role of a philosopher who believes in the dominant moral values of the eighteenth century and a bum (or beatnik) who denies all these values has had an extraordinary history. It first appeared in a German translation by Goethe in 1805; the full French text in Diderot's hand was not discovered until the end of the nineteenth century. The German philosopher Hegel was the first to recognize in *Rameau's Nephew* the perfect portrait of the "alienated man." We use the translation by John Morley from an appendix to his work *Diderot and the Encyclopaedists* (London, 1878).

He.—In nature, all species devour one another; so all ranks devour one another in society. We do justice on one another, without any meddling from the law. The other day it was Deschamps, now it is Guimard, who avenges the prince of the fiancier; and it is the milliner, the jeweller, the upholsterer, the hosier, the draper, the lady's-maid, the cook, the saddler, who avenge the financier of Deschamps. In the midst of it all, there is only the imbecile or the sloth who suffers injury without inflicting it. Whence you see that these exceptions to the general conscience, or these moral idioms about which they make such a stir, are nothing, after all, and that you only need to take a clear survey of the whole.

I.—I admire yours.

He.—And then misery! The voice of conscience and of honour is terribly weak, when the stomach calls out. Enough to say that if ever I grow rich I shall be bound to restore, and I have made up my mind to restore in every possible fashion, by eating, drinking, gambling, and whatever else you please.

I.—I have some fears about your ever growing rich.

He.—I have suspicions myself.

I.—But if things should fall so, what then?

He.—I would do like all other beggars set on horseback: I would be the most insolent ruffler that has ever been seen. Then I should recall all that they have made me go through, and should pay them back with good interest all the advances that they have been good enough to make me. I am fond of command, and I will command. I am fond of praise, and I will make them praise me. I will have in my pay the whole troop of flatterers, parasites, and buffoons, and I'll say to them, as has been said to me: "Come, knaves, let me be amused," and amused I shall be; "Pull me some honest folk to pieces," and so they will be, if honest folk can be found. We will be jolly over our cups, we have all sorts of vices and whimsies; it will be delicious. We will prove that Voltaire has no genius; that Buffon, everlastingly perched upon his stilts, is only a turgid declaimer; that Montesquieu is nothing more than a man with a touch of ingenuity; we will send D'Alembert packing to his fusty mathematics. We will welcome before and behind all the pigmy Catos like you, whose modesty is the prop of pride, and whose sobriety is a fine name for not being able to help yourselves.

I.—From the worthy use to which you would put your riches, I perceive what a pity it is that you are a beggar. You would live thus in a manner that would be eminently honourable to the human race, eminently useful to your countrymen, and eminently glorious for yourself.

He.—You are mocking me, sir philosopher. But you do not know whom you are laughing at. You do not suspect that at this moment I represent the most important part of the town and the court. Our millionaires in all ranks have, or have not, said to themselves exactly the same things as I have just confided to you; but the fact is, the life that I should lead is precisely their life. What a notion you people have; you think that the same sort of happiness is made for all the world. What a strange vision! Yours supposes a certain romantic spirit that we know nothing of, a singular character, a peculiar taste. You adorn this incongruous mixture with the name of philosophy; but now, are virtue and philosophy made for all the world? He has them who can get them, and he keeps them who can. Imagine the universe sage and philosophical; agree that it would be a most diabolically gloomy spot. Come, long live philosophy! The wisdom of Solomon forever! To drink good wines, to cram one's self with dainty dishes, to rest in beds of down: except that, all, all is vanity and vexation of spirit.

I.—What, to defend one's native land?

He.—Vanity; there is native land no more; I see nought from pole to pole but tyrants and slaves.

I.—To help one's friends?

He.—Vanity; has one any friends? If one had, ought we to turn them into ingrates? Look well, and you will see that this is all you get by doing services. Gratitude is a burden, and every burden is made to be shaken off.

I.—To have a position in society and fulfil its duties?

He.—Vanity; what matters it whether you have a position or not, provided you are rich, since you only seek a position to become rich? To fulfil one's duties, what does that lead to? To jealousy, trouble, persecution. Is that the way to get on? Nay indeed: to see the great, to court them, study their taste, bow to their fancies, serve their vices, praise their injustice—there is the secret.

I.—To watch the education of one's children?

He.—Vanity; that is a tutor's business.

I.—But if this tutor, having picked up his principles from you, happens to neglect his duties, who will pay the penalty?

He.—Not I, at any rate, but most likely the husband of my daughter, or the wife of my son.

I.—But suppose that they both plunge into vice and debauchery?

He.—That belongs to their position.

I.—Suppose they bring themselves into dishonour?

He.—You never come into dishonour, if you are rich, whatever you do.

I.—Suppose they ruin themselves?

He.—So much the worse for them.

I.—You will not pay much heed to your wife?

He.—None whatever, if you please. The best compliment, I think, that a man can pay his dearer half, is to do what pleases himself. In your opinion, would not society be mightly amusing, if everybody in it was always attending to his duties?

I.—Why not? The evening is never so fair to me, as when I am satisfied with my morning.

He.—And to me also.

I.—What makes the men of the world so dainty in their amusements, is their profound idleness.

He.—Pray do not think that; they are full of trouble.

I.—As they never tire themselves, they are never refreshed.

He.—Don't suppose that, either. They are incessantly worn out.

I.—Pleasure is always a business for them, never the satisfaction of a necessity.

He.—So much the better; necessity is always a trouble.

I.—They wear everything out. Their soul gets blunted, weariness seizes them. A man who should take their life in the midst of all their crushing abundance, would do them a kindness. The only part of happiness that they know is the part that loses its edge. I do not despise the pleasures of the senses: I have a palate, too, and it is tickled by a well-seasoned dish or a fine wine; I have a heart and eyes, and I like to see a handsome woman. Sometimes with my friends, a gay party, even if it waxes somewhat tumultuous, does not displease me. But I will not dissemble from you that it is infinitely pleasanter to me to have succoured the unfortunate, to have ended some thorny business, to have given wholesome counsel, done some pleasant reading, taken a walk with some man or woman dear to me, passed instructive hours with my children, written a good page, fulfilled the duties of my position, said to the woman that I love, a few soft things that bring her arm round my neck. I know actions which I would give all that I possess, to have done. *Mahomet* is a sublime work; I would a hundred times rather have got justice for the memory of the Calas. A person of my acquaintance fled to Carthagena; he was the younger son in a country where custom transfers all the property to the eldest. There he learns that his eldest brother, a petted son, after having despoiled his father and mother of all that they possessed, had driven them out of the castle, and that the poor old souls were languishing in indigence in some small country town. What does he do—this younger son who in consequence of the harsh treatment he had received at the hand of his parents had gone to seek his fortune far away? He sends them help; he makes haste to set his affairs in order, he returns with his riches, he restores his father and mother to their home, and finds husbands for his sisters. Ah, my dear Rameau, that man looked upon this period as the happiest in his life; he had tears in his eyes when he spoke to me of it, and even as I tell you the story, I feel my heart beat faster, and my tongue falter for sympathy

He.—Singular beings, you are!

I.—'Tis you who are beings much to be pitied, if you cannot imagine that one rises above one's lot, and that it is impossible to be unhappy under the shelter of good actions.

He.—That is a kind of felicity with which I should find it hard to familiarise myself, for we do not often come across it. But, then, according to you, we should be good.

I.—To be happy, assuredly.

He.—Yet I see an infinity of honest people who are not happy, and an infinity of people who are happy without being honest.

I.—You think so.

He.—And is it not for having had common sense and frankness for a moment, that I don't know where to go for a supper to-night?

I.—Nay, it is for not having had it always; it is because you did not perceive in good time that one ought first and foremost to provide a resource independent of servitude.

He.—Independent or not, the resource I had provided is at any rate the most comfortable.

I.—And the least sure and least decent.

He.—But the most conformable to my character of sloth, madman, and good-for-nought.

I.—Just so.

He.—And since I can secure my happiness by vices which are natural to me, which I have acquired without labour, which I preserve without effort, which go well with the manners of my nation, which are to the taste of those who protect me, and are more in harmony with their small private necessities, than virtues which would weary them by being a standing accusation against them from morning to night, why, it would be very singular for me to go and torment myself like a lost spirit, for the sake of making myself into somebody other than I am, to put on a character foreign to my own, and qualities which I will admit to be highly estimable, in order to avoid discussion, but which it would cost me a great deal to acquire, and a great deal to practise, and would lead to nothing, or possibly to worse than nothing, through the continual satire of the rich among whom beggars like me have to seek their subsistence.

We praise virtue, but we hate it, and shun it, and know very well that it freezes the marrow of our bones—and in this world one must have one's feet warm. And then all that would infallibly fill me with ill-humour; for why do we so constantly see religious people so harsh, so querulous, so unsociable? 'Tis because they have imposed a task upon themselves which is not natural to them. They suffer, and when people suffer, they make others suffer too. That is not my game, nor that of my protectors either; I have to be gay, supple, amusing, comical. Virtue makes itself respected, and respect is inconvenient; virtue insists on being admired, and admiration is not amusing. I have to do with people who are bored, and I must make them laugh. Now it is absurdity and madness which make people laugh, so mad and absurd I must be; and even if nature had not made me so, the simplest plan would still be to feign it. Happily, I have no need to play hypocrite; there are so many already of all colours, without reckoning those who play hypocrite with themselves. . . . If your friend Rameau were to apply himself to show his contempt for fortune, and women, and good cheer, and idleness, and to begin to Catonize, what would he be but a hypocrite? Rameau must be what he is—a lucky rascal among rascals swollen with riches, and not a mighty paragon of virtue, or even a virtuous man, eating his dry crust of bread, either alone, or by the side of a pack of beggars. And, to cut it short, I do not get on with your felicity, or with the happiness of a few visionaries like yourself.

I.—I see, my friend, that you do not even know what it is, and that you are not even made to understand it.

He.—So much the better, I declare; so much the better. It would make me burst with hunger and weariness, and maybe, with remorse.

I.—Very well, then, the only advice I have to give you, is to find your way back as quickly as you can into the house from which your impudence drove you out.

He.—And to do what you do not disapprove absolutely, and yet is a little repugnant to me relatively?

I.—What a singularity!

He.—Nothing singular in it at all; I wish to be abject, but I wish to be so without constraint. I do not object to descend from my dignity. . . . You laugh?

I.—Yes, your dignity makes me laugh.

He.—Everybody has his own dignity. I do not object to come down from mine, but it must be in my own way, and not at the bidding of others. Must they be able to say to me, Crawl—and behold me, forced to crawl? That is the worm's way, and it is mine; we both of us follow it—the worm and I—when they leave us alone, but we turn when they tread on our tails. They have trodden on my tail, and I mean to turn. And then you have no idea of the creature we are talking about. Imagine a sour and melancholy person, eaten up by vapours, wrapped twice or thrice round in his dressing-gown, discontented with himself, and discontented with everyone else; out of whom you hardly wring a smile, if you put your body and soul out of joint in a hundred different ways; who examines with a cold considering eye the droll grimaces of my face, and those of my mind, which are droller still. I may torment myself to attain the highest sublime of the lunatic asylum, nothing comes of it. Will he laugh, or will he not? That is what I am obliged to keep saying to myself in the midst of my contortions; and you may judge how damaging this uncertainty is to one's talent. My hypochondriac, with his head buried in a night-cap that covers his eyes, has the air of an immovable pagod, with a string tied to its chin, and going down under his chair. You wait for the string to be pulled, and it is not pulled; or if by chance the jaws open, it is only to articulate some word that shows he has not seen you, and that all your drolleries have been thrown away. This word is the answer to some question which you put to him four days before; the word spoken, the mastoid muscle contracts, and the jaw sticks.

[Then he set himself to imitate his man. He placed himself on a chair, his head fixed, his hat coming over his eyebrows, his eyes half-shut, his arms hanging down, moving his jaw up and down like an automaton:] Gloomy, obscure, oracular as destiny itself—such is our patron.

At the other side of the room is a prude who plays at importance, to whom one could bring one's self to say that she is pretty, because she is pretty, though she has a blemish or two upon her face. *Item,* she is more spiteful, more conceited, and more silly than a goose. *Item,* she insists on having wit. *Item,* you have to persuade her that you believe she has more of it than anybody else in the world. *Item,* she knows nothing, and she has a turn for settling everything out of hand. *Item,* you must applaud her decisions with feet and hands, jump for joy, and scream with admiration:—"How fine that is, how delicate, well said, subtly seen, singularly felt! Where do women get that? Without study, by mere force of instinct, and pure light of nature! That is really like a miracle! And then they want us to believe that experience, study, reflection, education, have anything to do with the matter! . . ." And other fooleries to match, and tears and tears of joy; ten times a day to kneel down, one knee bent in front of the other, the other leg drawn back, the arms extended towards the goddess, to seek one's desire in her eyes, to hang on her lips, to wait for her command, and then start off like a flash of lightning. Where is the man who would subject himself to play such a part, if it is not the wretch who finds there two or three times a week the wherewithal to still the tribulation of his inner parts?

5. Diderot: The Innocent and the Corrupt

Louis-Antoine de Bougainville conducted an expedition to the South Pacific, including Tahiti, from 1766 to 1769. Upon his return to France he gave an account of his explorations, which Diderot used in 1772 as a point of departure for contrasting the sexual customs and moral values of the natural man of Tahiti with those of the European. "The Old Man's Farewell (from *Supplement to Bougainville's 'Voyage'*) is a bitter indictment of Western civilization. During Diderot's lifetime this dialogue circulated in manuscript; it was not published until 1796. The translation is by Frank and Fritzie Manuel.

The speaker is an old man. He was the father of a large family. When the Europeans arrived he cast disdainful looks at them, without showing any signs of astonishment, fear, or curiosity. When they approached him he turned his back and retired into his hut. His silence and his worried look betrayed his thoughts all too clearly. Within him he lamented the passing of the happy days of his land. Upon Bougainville's departure, when the inhabitants rushed to the shore in a crowd, clung to his clothes, embraced his companions, and wept, this old man came forward with a serious mien and said,

"Weep, unfortunate Tahitians! Weep! But over the arrival, not the departure, of these ambitious and wicked men. Some day you will come to know them better. Some day they will return. With the piece of wood, which you see attached to this man's girdle in one hand, and in the other the sword which hangs by that one's side, they will come to put you in chains, to slaughter you, to subject you to their wild fantasies and to their vices. Some day you will be made to serve under them, after you have become as corrupt, as vile, and as miserable as they are. But I comfort myself. I am approaching the end of my life's span. And the calamity

99

which I predict for you, I shall never witness. O, Tahitians! O, my friends! You would have one way of escaping that disastrous future. But I would rather die than give you such advice. Let them go away, and let them live."

Then addressing himself to Bougainville he added, "And you, chief of the brigands who obey you. Quickly get your vessel away from our shores. We are innocent. We are happy. And you can only hurt our felicity. We follow the unsullied instinct of nature alone. And you have tried to erase its mark from our souls. Here everything belongs to everybody. And you have preached to us of I know not what distinction between *yours* and *mine*. We hold our daughters and our wives in common. You have shared this privilege with us. And you have come to ignite in them hitherto unknown frenzies. They have gone mad in your arms. You have become ferocious in theirs. They have begun to hate each other. You have cut each other's throats over them, and they have come back to us stained with your blood. We are free, and here you have implanted in our earth the standard proclaiming our future slavery. You are neither a god nor a demon. Who then are you to make slaves of others? Orou! You who understand the language of these men, tell all of us, as you told me, what they wrote on their plaque of metal. *This land is ours.* This land is yours! And why? Because you set foot on it? If a Tahitian disembarked one day on your shores and engraved on one of your stones or on the bark of your trees, *This land belongs to the inhabitants of Tahiti,* what would you think? You are stronger. And what of that? When someone took away from you one of the contemptible trinkets with which your ship is laden, you cried out, you avenged yourself. And in that very same moment you planned in the depth of your heart the theft of a whole country. You are not a slave. You would rather die than be one, and yet you want to subjugate us. Do you think then that the Tahitian does not know how to die in defence of his liberty? The Tahitian of whom you wish to take possession like an animal is your brother. You are two children of nature. What right do you have over him that he does not have over you? You came. Did we throw ourselves upon your person? Did we pillage your ship? Did we seize you and expose you to the arrows of our enemies? Did we bind you to the labor of our beasts in our fields? We have respected our image in you. Leave us to our customs. They are wiser and more honorable than yours. We would never trade what you call our ignorance for your useless knowledge. Everything that is necessary and good for us we possess. Are we worthy of contempt because we have not known how to create superfluous needs for ourselves? When we are hungry we have enough to eat. When we are cold we have something with which to cover ourselves. You have been in our huts. What, in your opinion, is lacking there? Pursue where you will what you call the comforts of life. But allow sensible beings to stop when they can obtain from the continuance of their painful efforts nothing but imaginary goods. If you persuade us to cross the narrow bounds of need when shall we finish working? When shall we enjoy ourselves? We have made the sum total of our annual and daily burdens as light as possible because nothing appears to us to be preferable to repose. Go agitate yourself in your own country, torment yourself as much as you like. Leave us in peace. Do not bother us either with your factitious needs or with your chimerical virtues. Look at these men. See how erect, healthy, and strong they are. Look at these women. See how erect, healthy, fresh, and beautiful they are. Take this bow, it is mine. Call to your aid one, two, three, four of your companions, and try to bend it. I can bend it alone. I work the soil. I climb the mountain. I penetrate the forest. I can cross a league of the open plain in less than an hour. Your young companions found it difficult to keep up with me. And I am more than ninety. Woe to this island. Woe to the living Tahitians of today and to all those who shall come after them, ever since you came to visit us! We used to know only one sickness. That to which man, animal, and plant were all condemned—old age. And you have brought us another. You have infected our blood. Perhaps we shall have to exterminate with our own hands our daughters, our wives, our children. Those who approached your women, those who approached your men. Our fields will be soaked with the impure blood which has passed from your veins into ours. Or our children will be condemned to nourish and to perpetuate the evil which you have given to their fathers and mothers and which they will transmit forever to their descendants. Wretch! You will be guilty either of the ravages which follow the fatal caresses of your kind or of the murders which we shall commit to stop the poison. You speak of crimes. Do you know of any greater one than yours? What is your punishment for one who kills his neighbor? Death by the sword. What is your punishment for the coward who poisons? Death by fire. Compare your crime to the latter and tell us, poisoner of peoples, the punishment which you deserve. It was only a moment ago that the young Tahitian girl abandoned herself with ecstasy to the kisses of the young Tahitian boy. She waited with impatience the moment when her mother, authorized by her coming of age, raised her veil and revealed her naked breast. She was proud to arouse desires and to excite the amorous glances of the stranger, of her relatives, of her brother. She accepted without fear and without shame, in our presence, amidst a group of innocent Tahitians, listening to the sound of the flutes, between dances, the caresses of the one whom her young heart and the secret voice of her senses designated for her. The idea of crime and the threat of illness came among us with your entry. Our pleasures, once so gentle, are now accompanied by remorse and by fear. This black man who is near you, who is listening to me, has spoken to our boys. I do not know what he has said to our girls. But our boys hesitate, our girls blush. Bury yourself if you like in the dark forest with the perverse partner of your pleasures, but let the good and simple Tahitians reproduce themselves without shame, under the open sky and in broad daylight. What more decent and nobler feeling could you substitute for that which we have instilled in them and which animates them. They think that the time has come to enrich the nation and the family with a new citizen, and they glory in it. They eat to live and to grow. They grow to multiply and they find neither vice nor shame in it. Listen to the consequences of your crimes. Hardly had you shown yourself among them than they became thieves. Hardly had you touched our land than it reeked with blood. The Tahitian who ran to meet you, who welcomed you, who received you with the cry, *Taio! friend, friend,* you have killed. And why have you killed him? Because he had been seduced by the brilliance of your little serpents' eggs. He gave you his fruits. He offered you his wife and his daughter. He turned over his hut to you. And you killed him for a handful of these beads which he took without asking you for them. And this people? Upon hearing the noise of your murderous weapon, terror seized them and they took refuge in the mountain. But believe me they would not have delayed long in coming down. Believe me that in an instant, without me, you would have perished. Eh! why did I pacify them? Why did I restrain them? Why do I still hold them back at this moment? I do not know. For you do not merit any feeling of pity. For you have a ferocious soul which will never experience it. You walked about on our island, you and yours. You were respected. You enjoyed everything. You found in your path neither barrier nor refusal. You were invited. You sat down. They spread before you the abundance of the land. Did you want young girls? Except for those who do not yet have the privilege of showing their face and their bosom, the mothers presented them to you stark naked. There you are possessor of the tender victim of the duty of hospitality. For her and for you they strewed the earth with leaves and flowers. The musicians tuned up their instruments. Nothing disturbed the sweetness nor troubled the freedom of your caresses and hers. They sang the hymn, the hymn which exhorted you to be a man, which exhorted our child to be a woman, and a compliant and a voluptuous woman. They danced around your couch. And it was upon leaving the arms of this woman, after having known on her breast the sweetest intoxication, that you killed her brother, her friend, her father perhaps. You did even worse. Look this way. See this enclosure bristling with arrows. These arms which had once threatened only our enemies, see them turned against our own children. Look at the unfortunate companions of your pleasures. Gaze upon this sadness. See the grief of their fathers, see the despair of their mothers. It is there that they are condemned to perish either at our hands or from the disease which you have given them. Go away, unless your cruel eyes take delight in scenes of death. Go away. Go and may the guilty seas which spared you on your voyage here, absolve themselves and avenge us by swallowing you up before your return. And you, Tahitians, go back to your huts, go in all of you. Let these unworthy foreigners hear upon their departure nothing but the roar of the waves and let them see nothing but the foam whose fury whitens a deserted shore."

Part Four

🎋 LIBERTY & JUSTICE

1. Montesquieu: Liberty of the Constitution and of the Subject

Well into the nineteenth century Books XI and XII of *The Spirit of the Laws* by Charles de Secondat, Baron de Montesquieu, served as guide-lines for liberal European consitution-makers and proponents of the rights of man in a free society. Montesquieu's rather roseate view of the state of political liberty in England created an image which inspired many peoples to imitate its constitution. Though the theory of "the division of powers" was not original with him, later discussions about the proper relations of the executive, legislative, and judicial branches of government tended to revolve around the propositions formulated in these books. The work first appeared in Geneva in 1748, and Thomas Nugent translated it into English in 1750. Our text is from the Edinburgh edition of 1772.

Of the End or View of Different Governments

Though all governments have the same general end, which is that of preservation, yet each has another particular view. Increase of dominion was the view of Rome; war, of Sparta; religion, of the Jewish laws; commerce, that of Marseilles; public tranquillity, that of the laws of China; navigation, that of the laws of Rhodes; natural liberty, that of the policy of the savages; in general, the pleasures of the prince that of despotic states; that of monarchies, the prince's and the kingdom's glory; the independence of individuals, is the end aimed at by the laws of Poland, and from thence results the oppression of the whole.

One nation there is also in the world, that has for the direct end of its constitution political liberty. We shall examine presently the principles on which this liberty is founded; if they are sound, liberty will appear as in a mirror.

To discover political liberty in a constitution, no great labor is requisite. If we are capable of seeing it where it exists, why should we go any further in search of it?

Of the Constitution of England

In every government there are three sorts of power; the legislative; the executive, in respect to things dependent on the law of nations; and the executive, in regard to things that depend on the civil law.

By virtue of the first, the prince or magistrate enacts temporary or perpetual laws, and amends or abrogates those that have been already enacted. By the second, he makes peace or war, sends or receives embassies; establishes the public security, and provides against invasions. By the third, he punishes criminals, or determines the disputes that arise between individuals. The latter we shall call the judiciary power, and the other simply the executive power of the state.

The political liberty of the subject is a tranquillity of mind, arising from the opinion each person has of his safety. In order to have this liberty, it is requisite the government be so constituted as one man need not be afraid of another.

When the legislative and executive powers are united in the same person, or in the same body of magistrates, there can be no liberty; because apprehensions may arise, lest the same monarch or senate should enact tyrannical laws, to execute them in a tyrannical manner.

Again, there is no liberty, if the power of judging be not separated from the legislative and executive powers. Were it joined with the legislative, the life and liberty of the subject would be exposed to arbitrary control; for the judge would then be the legislator. Were it joined to the executive power, the judge might behave with all the violence of an oppressor.

There would be an end of every thing, were the same man, or the same body, whether of the nobles or of the people to exercise those three powers, that of enacting laws, that of executing the public resolutions, and that of judging the crimes or differences of individuals.

Most kingdoms in Europe enjoy a moderate government, because the prince, who is invested with the two first powers, leaves the third to his subjects. In Turkey, where these three powers are united in the sultan's person, the subjects groan under the weight of a most frightful oppression.

In the republics of Italy, where these three powers are united, there is less liberty than in our monarchies. Hence their government is obliged to have recourse to as violent methods for its support, as even that of the Turks; witness the state inquisitors, and the lion's mouth into which every informer may at all hours throw his written accusations.

What a situation must the poor subject be in, under those republics! The same body of magistrates are possessed, as executors of the laws, of the whole power they have given themselves in quality of legislators. They may plunder the state by their general determinations; and as they have likewise the judiciary power in their hands, every private citizen may be ruined by their particular decisions.

The whole power is here united in one body; and though there is no external pomp that indicates a despotic sway, yet the people feel the effects of it every moment.

Hence it is that many of the princes of Europe, whose aim has been levelled at arbitrary power, have constantly set out with uniting in their own persons, all the branches of magistracy, and all the great offices of state.

The executive power ought to be in the hands of a monarch; because this branch of government, which has always need of expedition, is better administered by one than by many: Whereas, whatever depends on the legislative power, is oftentimes better regulated by many than by a single person.

But if there was no monarch, and the executive power was committed to a certain number of persons selected from the legislative body, there would be an end then of liberty; by reason the two powers would be united, as the same persons would actually sometimes have, and would moreover be always able to have, a share in both.

Were the legislative body to be a considerable time without meeting, this would likewise put an end to liberty. For one of these two things would naturally follow; either that there would be no longer any legislative resolutions, and then the state would fall into anarchy; or that these resolutions would be taken by the executive power, which would render it absolute.

It would be needless for the legislative body to continue always assembled. This would be troublesome to the representatives, and moreover would cut out too much work for the executive power, so as to take off its attention from executing, and oblige it to think only of defending its own prerogatives, and the right it has to execute.

Again, were the legislative body to be always assembled, it might happen to be kept up only by filling the places of the deceased members with new representatives; and in that case, if the legislative body was once corrupted, the evil would be past all remedy. When different legislative bodies succeed one another, the people who have a bad opinion of that which is actually sitting, may reasonably entertain some hopes of the next: But were it to be always the same body, the people, upon seeing it once corrupted, would no longer expect any good from its laws; and of course they would either become desperate, or fall into a state of indolence.

The legislative body should not assemble of itself. For a body is supposed to have no will but when it is assembled; and besides, were it not to assemble unanimously, it would be impossible to determine which was really the legislative body, the part assembled, or the other. And if it had a right to prorogue itself, it might happen never to be prorogued; which would be extremely dangerous, in case it should ever attempt to encroach on the executive power. Besides, there are seasons, some of which are more proper than others, for assembling the legislative body: It is fit therefore that the executive power should regulate the time of convening, as well as the duration of those assemblies, according to the circumstances and exigencies of state known to itself.

Were the executive power not to have a right of putting a stop to the encroachments of the legislative body, the latter would become despotic; for as it might arrogate to itself what authority it pleased, it would soon destroy all the other powers.

But it is not proper, on the other hand, that the legislative power should have a right to stop the executive. For as the execution has its natural limits, it is useless to confine it; besides, the executive power is generally employed in momentary operations. The power therefore of the Roman tribunes was faulty, as it put a stop not only to the legislation, but likewise to the execution itself; which was attended with infinite mischiefs.

But if the legislative power in a free government ought to have no right to stop the executive, it has a right, and ought to have the means of examining in what manner its laws have been executed; an advantage which this government has over that of Crete and Sparta, where the Cosmi and the Ephori gave no account of their administration.

But whatever may be the issue of that examination, the legislative body ought not to have a power of judging the person, nor of course the conduct of him who is intrusted with the executive power. His person should be sacred, because as it is necessary for the good of the state to prevent the legislative body from rendering themselves arbitrary, the moment he is accused or tried, there is an end of liberty.

To prevent the executive power from being able to oppress, it is requisite, that the armies, with which it is intrusted, should consist of the people, and have the same spirit as the people, as was the case at Rome, till the time of Marius. To obtain this end, there are only two ways, either that the persons employed in the army, should have sufficient property to answer for their conduct to their fellow subjects, and be enlisted only for a year, as customary at Rome: Or if there should be a standing army, composed chiefly of the most despicable part of the nation, the legislative power should have a right to disband them as soon as it pleased; the soldiers should live in common with the rest of the people; and no separate camp, barracks, or fortress, should be suffered.

When once an army is established, it ought not to depend immediately on the legislative, but on the executive power; and this from the very nature of the thing; its business consisting more in action than in deliberation.

From a manner of thinking that prevails amongst mankind, they set a higher value upon courage than timorousness, on activity than prudence, on strength than counsel. Hence, the army will ever despise a senate, and respect their own officers. They will naturally slight the orders sent them by a body of men, whom they look upon as cowards, and therefore unworthy to command them. So that as soon as the army depends on the legislative body, the government becomes a military one; and if the contrary has ever happened, it has been owing to some extraordinary circumstances. It is because the army was always kept divided; it is because it was composed of several bodies, that depended each on their particular province; it is because the capital towns were strong places, defended by their natural situation, and not garrisoned with regular troops. Holland, for instance, is still safer than Venice; she might drown, or starve the revolted troops; for as they are not quartered in towns capable of furnishing them with necessary subsistence, this subsistence is of course precarious.

Whoever shall read the admirable treatise of Tacitus on the manners of the Germans, will find that it is from them the English have borrowed the idea of their political government. This beautiful system was invented first in the woods.

As all human things have an end, the state we are speaking of will lose its liberty, it will perish. Have not Rome, Sparta, and Carthage perished? It will perish when the legislative power shall be more corrupted than the executive.

It is not my business to examine whether the English actually enjoy this liberty, or not. It is sufficient for my purpose to observe, that it is established by their laws; and I inquire no further.

Neither do I pretend by this to undervalue other governments, not to say that this extreme political liberty ought to give uneasiness to those who have only a moderate share of it. How should I have any such design, I who think that even the excess of reason is not always desirable, and that mankind generally find their account better in mediums than in extremes?

Of the Liberty of the Subject

Philosophical liberty consists in the free exercise of the will; or at least, if we must speak agreeable to all systems, in an opinion that we have the free exercise of our will. Political liberty consists in security, or at least in the opinion that we enjoy security.

This security is never more dangerously attacked than in public or private accusations. It is therefore on the goodness of criminal laws that the liberty of the subject principally depends.

Criminal laws did not receive their full perfection all at once. Even in places where liberty has been most sought after, it has not been always found. Aristotle informs us, that at Cumae the parents of the accuser might be witnesses. So imperfect was the law under the kings of Rome, that Servius Tullius pronounced sentence against the children of Ancus Marcius, who were charged with ing assassinated the king his father-in-law. Under the first kings of France, Clotarius made a law, that nobody should be condemned without being heard; which shews that a contrary custom had prevailed in some particular case, or among some barbarous people. It was Charondas that first established penalties against false witnesses. When the subject has no sence to secure his innocence, he has none for his liberty.

The knowledge already acquired in some countries, or that may be hereafter attained in others, in regard to the surest rules that can be observed in criminal judgments, is more interesting to mankind than any other thing in the universe.

Liberty can only be founded on the practice of this knowledge: And supposing a state to have the best laws imaginable in this respect, a person tried under that state, and condemned to be hanged the next day, would have much more liberty, than a bashaw enjoys in Turkey.

Those laws which condemn a man to death on the deposition of a single witness, are fatal to liberty. In right reason there should be two, because a witness who affirms, and the accused who denies, make an equal balance, and a third must incline the scale.

The Greeks and Romans required one voice more to condemn: But our French law insists upon two. The Greeks pretended that their custom was established by the gods; but this more justly may be said of ours.

That Liberty Is Favored by the Nature and Proportion of Punishments

Liberty is in its highest perfection, when criminal laws derive each punishment from the particular nature of the crime. There are then no arbitrary decisions; the punishment does not flow from the capriciousness of the legislator, but from the very nature of the thing; and man uses no violence to man.

There are four sorts of crimes. Those of the first species are prejudicial to religion, the second to morals, the third to the public tranquillity, and the fourth to the security of the subject. The punishments inflicted for these crimes ought to proceed from the nature of each of these species.

In the class of crimes that concern religion, I rank only those which attack it directly, such as all simple sacrileges. For, as to crimes that disturb the exercise of it, they are of the nature of those which prejudice the tranquillity or security of the subject, and ought to be referred to those classes.

In order to derive the punishment of simple sacrileges from the nature of the thing, it should consist in depriving people of the advantages conferred by religion, in expelling them out of the temples, in a temporary or perpetual exclusion from the society of the faithful, in shunning their preference, in execrations, detestations and conjurations.

In things that prejudice the tranquillity or security of the state, secret actions are subject to human jurisdiction. But in those which offend the Deity, where there is no public action, there can be no criminal matter; the whole passes betwixt man and God, who knows the measure and time of his vengeance. Now, if magis-

trates, confounding things, should inquire also into hidden sacrileges, this inquisition would be directed to a kind of action that
does not at all require it; the liberty of the subject would be subverted by arming the zeal of timorous, as well as of presumptuous
consciences against him.

The mischief arises from a notion which some people have entertained of revenging the cause of the Deity. But we must honor
the Deity, and leave him to avenge his own cause. In effect, were
we to be directed by such a notion, where would be the end of
punishments? If human laws are to avenge the cause of an infinite
Being, they will be directed by his infinity, and not by the ignorance
and caprice of man.

An historian of Provence relates a fact, which furnishes us with
an excellent description of the consequences that may arise in weak
capacities from this notion of avenging the Deity's cause. A Jew
was accused of having blasphemed against the blessed Virgin; and,
upon conviction, was condemned to be flayed alive. A strange
spectacle was then seen: Gentlemen masked, with knives in their
hands, ascended the scaffold, and drove away the executioner, in
order to be the avengers themselves of the honor of the blessed
Virgin—I do not here choose to anticipate the reflections of the
reader.

The second class consists of those crimes which are prejudicial
to morals. Such is the violation of public or private continency,
that is, of the policy directing the manner in which the pleasure
annexed to the union of bodies is to be enjoyed. The punishment
of those crimes ought to be also derived from the nature of the
thing; the privation of such advantages as society has attached to
the purity of morals—fines, shame, necessity of concealment, public infamy, expulsion from home and society, and in fine, all such
punishments as belong to a corrective jurisdiction, are sufficient to
repress the temerity of the two sexes. In effect, these things are
less founded on wickedness, than on the forgetting and despising
ourselves.

We speak here of none but crimes that relate merely to morals;
for as to those that are prejudicial to the public security, such as
rapes and ravishments, they belong to the fourth species.

The crimes of the third class are those that disturb the public tranquillity. The punishments ought therefore to be derived from the nature of the thing, and to be relative to this tranquillity; such as imprisonment, exile, corrections, and other like chastisements, proper for reclaiming turbulent spirits, and reducing them to the established order.

I confine those crimes that injure the public tranquillity to things that imply a single transgression against the civil administration: For as to those which, by disturbing the public tranquillity, attack at the same time the security of the subject, they ought to be ranked in the fourth class.

The punishments inflicted upon the latter crimes are such as are properly distinguished by that name. They are a kind of retaliation, by which society refuses security to a member, who has actually or intentionally deprived another of his security. These punishments are derived from the nature of the thing, founded on reason, and drawn from the very source of good and evil. A man deserves death when he has violated the security so far as to deprive, or attempt to deprive another man of his life. This punishment of death is the remedy; as it were, of a sick society. When there is a breach of security in respect to property, there may be some reasons for inflicting a capital punishment: But it would be perhaps much better, and more natural, that crimes committed against the security of property should be punished with the loss of property, and this ought indeed to be the case, if mens fortunes were common or equal. But as those who have no property are generally the readiest to attack the property of others, it has been found necessary, instead of a pecuniary, to substitute a corporal punishment.

All that I have here advanced, is founded in nature, and extremely favorable to the liberty of the subject.

2. Morelly: Laws for a Communist Society

Very little is known about Morelly—not even his Christian names. He represents the extreme radical minority among the *philosophes*. This proposed collection of laws for a communist society probably was known to Gracchus Babeuf whose *Conspiracy of the Equals* shook the Directorate in 1796-1797. *Nature's Code or the true spirit of its laws in all times neglected or misunderstood* first appeared in 1755 without a place of publication on the title-page. Fritzie P. Manuel has translated the introduction, the economic, agrarian, edile, and police laws from Gilbert Chinard's edition (Paris, 1950).

Source of the errors of Moralists ancient and modern: how they could have recognized and avoided them.

I have tried to reveal this first link in the chain of error, and to make evident this first Point of deviation which has always kept our Moralists and Law-makers distant from the truth. Listen to the lot of them, they will posit for you as an indisputable principle and the foundation of all their systems the following important proposition: *Man is born vicious and wicked*. Not quite, some of them say, but the circumstances of life in this world, his very make-up, inevitably predispose him to perverseness. Accepting this in its most literal sense, none of them imagined that it could be otherwise; thus it did not occur to anyone to propound and resolve this splendid Problem:

To find a situation in which it would be almost impossible for man to be depraved, or wicked, or at least where there would be as little evil as possible.

Failing to formulate or solve this Problem, our Instructors among the ancients lost sight of the one first cause of all evil, the one obvious means which would have disclosed an initial error. Proceeding along the same path, our Moderns found themselves still further from a first truth which would have made them perceive clearly the real origin, nature, and lineage of the vices, and the ineffectiveness of the remedies which common Morality claims to apply to them. With the aid of this insight, I say, they could easily have dissected the official Morality, and proved that its hypotheses were false, its precepts ineffectual, its maxims contradictory, and its means opposed to their avowed ends; in short, demonstrated in detail the flaws in every portion of this monstrous corpus.

As with mathematical Equations, such Reasoning, avoiding and eliminating the false and the dubious, would finally make the *unknown quantity* emerge, that is, a System of Ethics truly susceptible of the clearest proofs.

Following this method, I found that in every age our Wise Men, who sought a cure for the corruption which they alas regarded as an inevitable attribute of the human condition, have begun by imagining the cause of that decay where it never resided, and should have taken as a remedy for the evil precisely that poison which they claimed was its cause.

None of these chatterboxes, who repeated themselves endlessly, ever thought of suspecting that the cause of man's corruption was in fact one of their first lessons; the substance appeared to them too pure, too noble for that; their laws, their regulations, too wise and estimable for anyone to dare lay this profound grievance at their door; they preferred to throw the blame on nature. And so man as they fashioned him, though completely wanting in metaphysical and moral ideas alike, simply equipped with the proper faculties to receive these ideas, man in the first moments of his existence, in truth totally insensitive to every impulse rather than excited to some impetuous passion, is, according to most of our Philosophers, pretty well endowed with a number of vices mixed with a few *innate* virtues along with ideas of the same ilk. Even before seeing the light of day, he carries in his breast the fatal seeds of corruption which will move him to seek his own good at the expense of the whole species and the entire universe if possible.

Were I to overlook that specious absurdity, I would still be right to point out that, far from seeking means to uproot or repress these wicked proclivities and so permit the burgeoning of a few fragile virtues whose roots, according to the learned Doctors, are not completely rotten; far, I say, from encouraging these wholesome inclinations, they have done precisely everything needed to plant the seed of vice in the heart of man and make it sprout—vice that was never there—and to suffocate in him the bit of virtue that they fancy they are cultivating.

Model legislation in accord with Nature's design.

I am giving this outline of Laws by way of an Appendix and as an excursus, since unfortunately it is only too true that in our day it would be practically impossible to establish such a Republic.

On the basis of this text, which needs no long commentaries, every intelligent Reader will be able to judge from how much distress these Laws would deliver men. I have just shown that it would have been easy for the first Legislators to act so that the Peoples of the earth knew no other laws: if my proofs are convincing my object is achieved.

I am not so rash as to pretend to reform human-kind; but I have courage enough to tell the truth, without concerning myself over the outcries of those who are afraid of it because they are interested in deluding our species or in abandoning it to the errors by which they themselves have been duped.

Fundamental and Sacred Laws

*Which would cut off at the root the vices and
all the evils of Society.*

I

Nobody will own anything in the Society individually or as an estate, except the things which he is currently using for his needs, his pleasures, or his daily work.

II

Every Citizen will be a public person, supported, maintained, and employed at Public expense.

III

For his part every Citizen will contribute to the public weal in accordance with his strength, his talents, and his age; these will determine his obligations, in conformity with the Distributive Laws.

DISTRIBUTIVE OR ECONOMIC LAWS

I

In order that everything may be carried out in an orderly fashion, without confusion or dispute, an entire Nation will be counted and divided into Families, Tribes, and Cities, and if its population is very large into Provinces.

II

Each Tribe will consist of the same number of Families, each City of the same number of Tribes, and so on.

III

As the Nation grows in population, the Tribes and Cities will be proportionately increased, but only until the increment is sufficient to form new Cities with as many persons as the others.

IV

All civil divisions involving things or persons will be made in terms of the number *ten* and its multiples; that is to say, all enumerations, every distribution by groups, every distributive measurement, etc., will consist of decimal parts.

V

On the basis of *tens* or *hundreds,* etc. of Citizens, there will be in each Occupation a number of Workers in proportion to the difficulty of their labor and what they will need to supply to the People of each City, without wearing themselves out.

VI

To regulate the distribution of the products of Nature and Art, it will be noted first that there are some *durable* things, that is, those which can be preserved or used a long time, and that among all the products of that sort there are: 1. those of daily and universal use; 2. That there are those of universal, but not continual use; 3. Some are continually necessary only to someone, and from time to time to everyone; 4. Others are never of continual or general use, such as those catering simply to pleasure or individual taste. Now, all these durable products will be collected in public warehouses for distribution, some daily or at stated times to all Citizens, for the ordinary needs of life and for carrying on their various Occupations; others will be supplied to people who make use of them.

VII

It will be noted in the second place that there are products of Nature or Art which are non-durable; these things will be brought to the marketplace and distributed by those who are in charge of cultivating or preparing them.

VIII

These products of every kind will be counted, and their quantities will be adapted either to the number of Citizens in each City, or to the number of those who use them: among the products, those which can be preserved will, according to the same rules, be publicly allotted, and their surplus held in reserve.

IX

If there should be a deficit of luxury items of universal or particular use, so that a single Citizen would be deprived, all distribution will be suspended, or else such items will be supplied only in the tiniest amount, until the insufficiency will have been remedied; but great care will be exercised that such accidents do not befall things which are universally necessary.

X

The surplus provisions of each City, of each Province, will be channeled into those who face a shortage, or will be reserved for future needs.

XI

According to *the sacred Laws,* nothing will be sold or bartered among Fellow-Citizens; thus, if anyone needs some herbs, vegetables, or fruits, he will go and take what he requires for one day only at the marketplace, where things are brought by those who grow them. If someone needs bread, he will go and get a supply sufficient for a certain length of time from the man who makes it, and the latter will find in the public warehouse the flour he needs for the amount of bread he is obliged to prepare for one or several days. The person who needs a piece of clothing will get it from him who fashions it, and he in turn will take the fabric from the one who makes it, and he will get the raw material from the warehouse where it will have been brought by those who gather it; and thus with everything else which will be distributed to each Head of a Family for his use and that of his Children.

XII

If a Nation succours a neighboring or foreign Nation with the products of its Countryside, this commerce alone will be effected through exchange and through the intermediary of Citizens who will declare everything publicly; but scrupulous care will be taken to see that such commerce does not introduce any private property into the Republic, even the slightest amount.

AGRARIAN LAWS

I

The territory of each city will be as compact and regular as possible, not to form a landed estate, but just adequate for the subsistence of its Inhabitants and the employment of those responsible for cultivating the Soil.

II

If a City happens to be located on barren land, only the Arts will be practiced there, and neighboring Cities will provide subsistence for its Inhabitants. Nevertheless that City, like the others, will have its *Farm corps,* either to make its land yield as much as possible, or to help in cultivating the lands of neighbor Cities.

III

Every Citizen, without exception, from the age of twenty to twenty-five, will be obliged to work at Farming, unless some infirmity excuses him from it.

IV

In each City this Agricultural Youth Corps will be composed of Laborers, Gardeners, Shepherds, Woodcutters, Pioneers, Wagoners and Boatmen, Carpenters, Masons, Blacksmiths, and other workmen in Building Trades. Young people who have worked in one of the first Capacities will be able to quit after a stated period and resume whatever they had previously been trained for, or remain in Agriculture as long as their strength permits.

Edile Laws

I

As in each City the Tribes will not exceed, or hardly, a certain number of Families, and as the Tribes will never exceed a certain number by more than one, all the Cities will have about the same extent.

II

Around a great Square of regular shape, buildings of uniform and attractive style will be erected; these will be the public Warehouses for all provisions, and the public meeting halls.

III

The Quarters of the City will extend in regular fashion from this enclosure; they will be of equal dimensions and shape, and regularly divided by Streets.

IV

Each Tribe will occupy a Quarter, and each Family a spacious and comfortable dwelling; all these buildings will be alike.

V

All the Quarters of a City will be so arranged that they can be enlarged if necessary without disturbing the regularity; such increases will not exceed definite limits.

VI

Some distance away and forming galleries around the Quarters of the City will be the workshops in all the mechanical Trades for all Work Corps whose number is greater than ten; for it was provided in *Distributive Law V* that in each City there would be only a sufficient number of Workers for every mechanical Trade.

VII

Outside this ring of workshops will be constructed another row of buildings designed to house persons employed in Agriculture and its dependent Occupations. The buildings will also be used as workshops for these Occupations, as Barns, Store-rooms, Mangers, Toolsheds, always accommodated to the needs of the particular City.

VIII

At some distance beyond all these circles, a spacious and commodious building will be put up on the most healthful site. In it any sick Citizen will find lodging and care.

IX

On another side there will be a comfortable shelter for all infirm and decrepit Citizens.

X

On another side, in the least agreeable and most deserted spot, a building will be constructed that is surrounded by high walls and is divided into several small dwellings, closed with iron railings. Here will be locked up those who deserve to be isolated from society for a time.

XI

Nearby will be the walled cemetery, which will hold individual buildings of very strong stonework, a type of cavern that is rather spacious and heavily barred, to shut in forever and then entomb Citizens who deserve Civil death, that is, to be forever excluded from Society. *See the Penal Laws.*

XII

In each City all buildings in general will be constructed, maintained, or rebuilt by the Work Corps assigned to Architecture.

XIII

The cleanliness of the Cities and of the public thoroughfares will ordinarily be maintained by the Pioneers and Drivers Corps; they will also be responsible for provisioning the warehouses and arranging their goods; when there is some extraordinary need all those who are occupied strictly with tilling the soil help out the others by putting in some work on the construction or repair of the public roads and on the aqueducts.

POLICE LAWS

I

In all Occupations the oldest and at the same time most experienced will take their turn in accordance with seniority in directing five or ten of their comrades for five days; and these supervisors will distribute their own work load fairly among the others.

II

In each Occupational Corps there will be a Master for ten or twenty Workers, whose task it will be to train them, to inspect their work, and to report on their diligence and conduct to the Corps Chief, who will hold office for a year; the Masters will be permanent, and will take turns at Corps Chief.

III

No one can be a Master until a year has elapsed after he finishes his Agricultural Service and returns to his first Occupation, in other words, until the end of his twenty-sixth year.

IV

In any Occupation, a person who makes an important discovery will share it with all the members of his Corps, and thenceforward he will be a Master even if he has not yet reached the proper age, and he will be designated Corps Chief for the following year; the rotation will be interrupted only in this case and will be resumed thereafter.

V

At the age of ten every Citizen will begin to learn the Occupation for which he feels some inclination and which he seems capable of performing, without being pushed into it; at fifteen or eighteen he will marry; from twenty to twenty-five he will be engaged in some branch of Farming; at twenty-six he will be a Master, in his first Trade if he resumes it, or if he continues to practice some Trade connected with Agriculture. But if he happens to embrace any other sort of occupation, then he can be a Master only at the age of thirty. At forty, every Citizen who has never been convicted of a crime will become a Voluntary Worker; that is, without being exempt from work, he wil be able to choose to whom he is subordinate, and will perform only the tasks which he sets for himself; he will be master of his hours of repose.

VI

The infirm and decrepit aged will be comfortably lodged, fed, and maintained in the public Shelter provided for that purpose in each City by *Edile Law IX*. All sick Citizens, without exception, will also be moved to the common residence that has been reserved for them, and will be cared for with the same meticulousness and cleanliness as in the bosom of their Families, and without distinction or preference. The Senate of each Town will be particularly concerned with proper management and service in these Houses, and will see to it that they are not wanting in anything necessary or agreeable, whether for the restoration of health, the progress of convalescence, or finally to while away the tedium of infirmity.

VII

The Chiefs of all the Trades will fix the hours of rest and of work, and will prescribe what is to be done.

VIII

Every fifth day will be set aside as a public day of rest; for that purpose the year will be divided into seventy-three equal parts; there will be a double day of rest only once in the year, to which a day should be added.

IX

Public celebrations will always begin on a public rest-day and will last a total of six days.

X

These celebrations will take place just before ploughing begins, before the harvest starts, after the gathering and stacking of fruits of all sorts, and at New Year's; on this last occasion marriages will be solemnized, and City and Corps Chiefs will take office.

3. Rousseau: The Origin of the Social Compact

The idea that the state was neither of patriarchal nor of divine origin but was based upon a contract among equals in a state of nature is one of those intellectual conceptions which reverberate for centuries after their initial utterance. Jean-Jacques Rousseau's *Treatise on the Social Compact: or, the Principles of Political Law* may no longer be an active force in Western European countries, but its eloquence and argument have moved men in the politically "less developed" parts of the world well into our own time. It first appeared in 1762 and was translated into English two years later. We quote from the early chapters (London, 1795).

Man is born free, and yet is universally enslaved. At the same time an individual frequently conceives himself to be the lord and master over others, though only more eminently deprived of liberty. Whence can this change arise? Are there any means by which it may be rendered lawful? The former question I cannot answer, though I imagine myself capable of resolving the latter.

If I took into consideration only the existence and effects of power, I should say, So long as a people are compelled to obey, they do well to be obedient; but, as soon as they are in a capacity to resist, they do better to throw off the yoke of restraint: for, in recovering their liberty on the same plea by which they lost it, either they have a just right to reassume it, or those could have none who deprived them of it. But there is an inviolable right founded on the very nature of society, which serves as the basis of all others. Man doth not derive this right, however, immediately from nature; it is founded on mutual convention. We must proceed, then, to inquire, of what kind such convention must have been. But, before we come to argue this point, I should establish what I have already advanced.

On the Primitive State of Society

The most ancient of all societies, and the only natural one, is that of a family. And even in this, children are no longer connected with their father than while they stand in need of his assistance. When this become needless, the natural tie is of course dissolved; the children are exempted from the obedience they owe their father, and the father is equally so from the solicitude due from him to his children; both assume a state of independence respecting each other. They may continue, indeed, to live together afterwards; but their connection, in such a case, is no longer natural, but voluntary; and even the family union is then maintained by mutual convention.

This liberty, which is common to all mankind, is the necessary consequence of our very nature; whose first law being that of self-preservation, our principal concerns are those which relate to ourselves: no sooner, therefore, doth man arrive at years of discretion, than he becomes the only proper judge of the means of that preservation, and of course his own master.

In a family, then, we may see the first model of political societies: their chief is represented by the father, and the people by his children, while all of them being free, and equal by birth, they cannot alienate their liberty, but for their common interest. All the difference between a family and a state lies in this, That, in the former, the love which a father naturally bears to his children is a compensation for his solicitude concerning them; and in the latter, it is the pleasure of command that supplies the place of this love, which a chief doth not entertain for his people.

Grotius denies that government is invested with power solely for the benefit of those who are governed, and cites the case of slaves as an example. It is, indeed, his constant practice to establish the matter of right on the matter of fact. He might have employed a more conclusive method, though not a more favourable one for tyrannical governments.

It is then doubtful, according to Grotius, whether the whole race of mankind, except about an hundred individuals, belong to those individuals, or whether the latter belong to the whole race of mankind; and he appears throughout his whole work, to lean to the former opinion. This is also the opinion of Hobbes. Thus they divide the human species into herds of cattle; each of which hath its keeper, who protects it from others only that he may make a property of it himself.

As a shepherd is of a superior nature to his flock; so the herd-keepers of men, or of their chiefs, are of a superior nature to the herd over which they preside. Such was the reasoning, according to Philo, of the Emperor Caligula; who concluded logically enough from this analogy, that either kings were gods, or their subjects no better than brutes.

This argument of Caligula bears much resemblance to those of Hobbes and Grotius. Aristotle has said, indeed, before either of them, that men were not naturally equal; but that some of them were born to slavery, and others to dominion.

Aristotle was right as to the fact, but mistook the effect for the cause. Nothing is more certain, than that every man born in slavery is born to be a slave. In such a state, men lose even the desire of freedom; and prefer subjection, as the companions of Ulysses did their brutality. If there are any slaves, therefore, by nature, it is because they are slaves contrary to nature. Power first made slaves, and cowardice hath perpetuated them.

I have said nothing of king Adam, or the emperor Noah, father of three monarchs, who like the children of Saturn, as some have imagined them to be, divided the world among them. I hope my moderation also in this respect will be esteemed some merit; for, as I am descended in a right line from one of these princes, and probably from the eldest branch of the family, how do I know, that, by a regular deduction of my descent, I might not find myself the legitimate heir to universal monarchy? Be this, however, as it may, it cannot be denied, that Adam had as good a title to the sovereignty of the world when he was the only person in it, as Robinson Crusoe had to that of his island under the same circumstances. A very great conveniency also attended their government, in that the monarch might rest securely on his throne, without fear of wars, conspiracies, or rebellion.

On the Right of the Strongest

The strongest is not strong enough to continue always master, unless he transforms his power into a right of command, and obedience into a duty. Hence is deduced the right of the strongest; a right taken ironically in appearance, and laid down as an established principle in reality. But will this term never be rightly explained? Force, in the simplest sense, is a physical power; nor can I see what morality can result from its effects. To yield to superior force is an act of necessity, not of the will, at most it is but an act of prudence. And in what sense can this be called a duty?

Let us suppose, however, for a moment, this pretended right established, and we shall see it attended with inexplicable absurdities: for if it be admitted that power constitutes right, the effect changes with the cause, and every succeeding power, if greater than the former, succeeds also to the right: so that men may lawfully disobey, as soon as they can do it with impunity; and, as right is always on the strongest side, they have nothing more to do, than to acquire superior force. Now what kind of right can that be, which vanishes with the power of enforcing it? If obedience be only exacted by compulsion, there is no need to make such obedience a duty; as when we are no longer compelled to obey, we are no longer obliged to it. It appears, therefore, that the word *right* adds nothing in this case to that of force, and in fact is a term of no signification.

Be obedient to the higher powers. If by this precept is meant, *subject to a superior force,* the advice is good, though superfluous; I will answer for it, such a rule will never be broken. All power, I own, is derived from God: but every corporeal malady is derived also from the same source. But are we therefore forbid to call in the physician? If a robber should stop me on the highway, am I not obliged, on compulsion, to give him my purse, but am I also obliged to it in point of conscience, though I might possibly conceal it from him? This will hardly be averred; and yet the pistol he holds to my breast is in effect a superior force.

On the whole, we must conclude, then, that mere power doth not constitute right, and that men are obliged only to pay obedience to lawful authority. Thus we are constantly recurring to my first question.

On Slavery

As no man hath any natural authority over the rest of his species, and as power doth not confer right, the basis of all lawful authority is laid in mutual convention.

If an individual, says Grotius, can alienate his liberty, and become the slave of a master, why may not a whole people collectively alienate theirs, and become subject to a king? This proposition, however, contains some equivocal terms, which require explanation; but I shall confine myself to that of *alienate*. Whatever is alienated must be disposed of, either by gift or sale. Now a man who becomes the slave of another, doth not give himself away; but sells himself, at least for his subsistence. But why should a whole people sell themselves? So far is a king from furnishing his subjects subsistence, that they maintain him; and, as our friend Rabelais says, a king doth not live on a little. Can subjects be supposed to give away their liberty, on condition that the receiver shall take their property along with it? After this, I really cannot see any thing they have left.

It may be said, a monarch maintains among his subjects the public tranquillity. Be it so; I would be glad to know of what they are gainers, if the wars in which his ambition engages them, if his insatiable avarice, or the oppressions of his ministers, are more destructive than civil dissensions? Of what are they gainers, if even this tranquillity be one cause of their misery? A prisoner may live tranquil enough in his dungeon; but will this be sufficient to make him contented there? When the Greeks were shut up in the cave of the Cyclops, they lived there unmolested, in expectation of their turn to be devoured.

To say that a man can give himself away, is to talk unintelligibly and absurdly; such an act must necessarily be illegal and void, were it for no other reason than that it argues insanity of mind in the agent. To say the same thing of a whole people therefore, is to suppose a whole nation can be at once out of their senses; but were it so, such madness could not confer right.

Were it possible also for a man to alienate himself, he could not in the same manner dispose of his children, who, as human beings, are born free; their freedom is their own, and nobody has a right to dispose of it but themselves. Before they arrive at years of discretion, indeed, their father may, for their security, and in their name, stipulate the conditions of their preservation; but he cannot unconditionally and irrevocably dispose of their persons; such a gift being contrary to the intention of nature, and exceeding the bounds of paternal authority. It is requisite, therefore, in order to render an arbitrary government lawful, that every new generation should be at liberty to admit or reject its authority, in which case it would be no longer an arbitrary government.

To renounce one's natural liberty, is to renounce one's very being as a man; it is to renounce not only the rights, but even the duties of humanity. And what possible indemnification can be made the man who thus gives up his all? Such a renunciation is incompatible with our very nature; for to deprive us of the liberty of the will, is to take away all morality from our actions. In a word, a convention, which stipulates on the one part absolute authority, and on the other implicit obedience, is in itself futile and contradictory. Is it not evident, that we can lie under no reciprocal obligation whatever to a person of whom we have a right to demand every thing? and doth not this circumstance, against which he has no equivalent, necessarily infer such act of convention to be void? For what claim can my slave have upon me, when he himself, and all that belongs to him, are mine? His claims are of course my own; and to say those can be set up against me, is to talk absurdly.

Again, Grotius and others have deduced the origin of this pretended right from the superiority obtained in war. The conqueror, say they, having a right to put the vanquished to death, the latter may equitably purchase his life at the expence of his liberty; such an agreement being the more lawful, as it conduces to the mutual advantage of both parties.

It is clear and certain, however, that this pretended right of the victor over the lives of the vanquished is not, in any shape, the natural result of a state of war. This is plain, were it for no other reason than that the reciprocal relations of mankind, while living together in their primitive independence, were not sufficiently durable to constitute a state either of peace or war; so that men cannot be naturally enemies. It is the relation subsisting between things, and not between men, that gives rise to war; which arising thus, not from personal, but real, relations, cannot subsist between man and man, either in a state of nature, in which there is no settled property, or in a state of society, in which every thing is secured by the laws.

The quarrels, encounters, and duels of individuals, are not sufficient to constitute such a state of war; and, with regard to the particular combats authorised by the institutions of Lewis XI, king of France; they were only some of the abuses of the feudal government; a system truly absurd, as contrary to the principles of natural justice, as of good policy.

War, is not, therefore, any relation between man and man, but a relation between state and state; in which individuals are enemies only accidentally, not as men, or even as citizens, but as soldiers; not as members of their particular community, but as its defenders. In short, a state can have for its enemy nothing but a state, not men; as between things essentially different there can be no common relation.

This principle is, indeed, conformable to the established maxims of all ages, and the constant practice of every civilized people. Declarations of war are made less to give notice to sovereigns, than to their subjects.

The foreigner, whether a sovereign, an individual, or a people, who plunders, kills, or takes prisoner a subject, without declaring war against his prince, is not an enemy, but a robber. Even in a time of war, a just prince may make himself master, in an enemy's country, of whatever belongs to the public; but he will respect the persons and private properties of individuals, he will respect those rights on which his own are founded. The design of war being the destruction of an hostile state, we have a right to kill its defenders while they are in arms; but as, in laying down their arms, they cease to be enemies, or instruments of hostility, they become in that case mere men, and we have not the least right to murder them.

It is sometimes possible effectually to destroy a state, without killing even one of its members; now, war cannot confer any right or privilege, which is not necessary to accomplish its end and design. It is true, these are not the principles of Grotius, nor are they founded on the authority of the poets; but they are such as are deduced from the nature of things, and are founded on reason.

With regard to the right of conquest, it has no other foundation than that of force, the law of the strongest. But, if war doth not give the victor a right to massacre the vanquished, this pretended right, which does not exist, cannot be the foundation of a right to enslave them. If we have no right to kill an enemy unless we cannot by force reduce him to slavery, our right to make him a slave never can be founded on our right to kill him. It is, therefore, an iniquitous bargain, to make him purchase, at the expence of liberty, a life, which we have no right to take away. In establishing thus a right of life and death over others, on that of enslaving them; and, on the other hand, a right of enslaving them on that of life and death; we certainly fall into the absurdity of reasoning in a circle.

Let us suppose, however, that this shocking right of general massacre existed, I still affirm, that a slave, made so by the fortune of war, or a conquered people, so reduced to slavery, lie under no other obligations to their master, than to obey him so long as he hath the power to compel them to it. In accepting of an equivalent for their lives, the victor confers on them no favour; instead of killing them uselessly, he hath only varied the mode of their destruction to his own advantage. So far, therefore, from his having acquired over them any additional authority, the state of war subsists between them as before; their relation to each other is the evident effect of it, and his exertion of the rights as of war is a proof, that no treaty of peace hath succeeded. Will it be said, they have made a convention? Be it so: this convention is a mere truce; and is so far from putting an end to the state of war, that it necessarily implies its continuation.

Thus, in whatever light we consider this affair, the right of making men slaves is null and void, not only because it is unjust, but because it is absurd and insignificant. The terms *slavery* and *justice* are contradictory, and reciprocally, exclusive of each other. Hence the following proposal would be equally ridiculous, whether made by one individual to another, or by a private man to a whole people. *I enter into an agreement with you, altogether at your own charge, and solely for my profit, which I will observe as long as I please, and which you are to observe also as long as I think proper.*

On the necessity of recurring always to the primitive convention

On the supposition that I should grant to be true what I have hitherto disproved, the advocate for despotism would, however, profit but little. There will be always a great difference between subjecting a multitude, and governing a society. Let individuals, in any number whatever, become severally and successively subject to one man, they are all, in that case, nothing more than master and slaves; they are not a people governed by their chiefs; they are an aggregate if you will, but do not form an association; there subsists among them neither commonwealth nor body-politic. Such a superior, though he should become the master of half the world, would be still a private person, and his interest, separate and distinct from that of his people, would be still no more than a private interest. When such a person dies, also, the empire over which he presided is dissolved, and its component parts remain totally unconnected, just as an oak falls into a heap of ashes when it is consumed by the fire.

A person, says Grotius, may voluntarily bestow themselves on a king: according to Grotius, therefore, a people are a people before they thus give themselves up to a regal authority. Even this gift, however, is an act of society, and presupposes a public deliberation on the matter. Hence, before we examine into the act by which a people make choice of a king, it is proper to examine into that by which a people became a people; for on this, which is necessarily prior to the other, rests the true foundation of society.

For, if in fact there be no prior convention, whence arises (unless indeed the election was unanimous) the obligation of the smaller number to submit to the choice of the greater? and whence comes it, that an hundred persons, for instance, who might desire to have a master, had a right to vote for ten others who might desire to have none? The choice by a plurality of votes is itself an establishment of convention, and supposes that unanimity must at least for once have subsisted among them.

On the social pact or covenant

      I suppose mankind arrived at that term when the obstacles to their preservation, in a state of nature, prevail over the endeavours of individuals to maintain themselves in such a state. At such a crisis this primitive state therefore could no longer subsist, and the human race must have perished if they had not changed their manner of living.

      Now as men cannot create new powers, but only compound and direct those which really exist, they have no other means of preservation, than that of forming, by their union, an accumulation of forces sufficient to oppose the obstacles to their security, and of putting these in action by a first mover capable of making them act in concert with each other.

      This general accumulation of power cannot arise but from the concurrence of many particular forces; but the force and liberty of each individual being the principal instruments of his own preservation, how is he to engage them in the common interest, without hurting his own, and neglecting the obligations he lies under to himself? This difficulty, being applied to my present subject, may be expressed in the following terms:

      "To find that form of association which shall protect and defend, with the whole force of the community, the person and property of each individual; and in which each person, by uniting himself to the rest, shall nevertheless be obedient only to himself, and remain as fully at liberty as before." Such is the fundamental problem, of which the Social Compact gives the solution.

      The clauses of this compact are so precisely determined by the nature of the act, that the least restriction or modification renders them void and of no effect; in so much, that although they may perhaps never have been formerly promulgated, they are yet universally the same, and are every where tacitly acknowledged and received. When the social pact, however, is violated, individuals recover their natural liberty, and are re-invested with their original rights, by losing that conventional liberty for the sake of which they had renounced them.

Again; these clauses, well understood, are all reducible to one, *viz.* the total alienation of every individual, with all his rights and privileges, to the whole community. For, in the first place, as every one gives himself up entirely and without reserve, all are in the same circumstances, so that no one can be interested in making their common connection burthensome to others.

Besides, as the alienation is made without reserve, the union is as perfect as possible, nor hath any particular associate any thing to reclaim; whereas, if they should severally retain any peculiar privileges, there being no common umpire to determine between them and the public, each being his own judge in some cases, would in time pretend to be so in all, the state of nature would still subsist, and their association would necessarily become tyrannical or void.

In fine, the individual, by giving himself up to all, gives himself to none; and as he acquires the same right over every other person in the community, as he gives them over himself, he gains an equivalent for what he bestows, and still a greater power to preserve what he retains.

If therefore we take from the Social Compact every thing that is not essential to it, we shall find it reduced to the following terms: "We, the contracting parties, do jointly and severally submit our persons and abilities to the supreme direction of the general will of all; and in a collective body, receive each member into that body as an indivisible part of the whole."

This act of association accordingly converts the several individual contracting parties into one moral collective body, composed of as many members as there are votes in the assembly, which receives also from the same act its unity and existence. This public personage, which is thus formed by the union of all its members, used formerly to be denominated a CITY, and at present takes the name of a *republic* or *body-politic*. It is also called, by its several members, a *state,* when it is passive; the *sovereign,* when it is active; and simply a *power,* when it is compared with other bodies of the same nature. With regard to the associates themselves, they take collectively the name of the *people;* and are separately called *citizens,* as partaking of the sovereign authority; and *subjects,* as subjected to the laws of the state. These terms, indeed, are frequently confounded, and mistaken one for the other; it is sufficient, however, to be able to distinguish them when they are to be used with precision.

4. Beccaria: The Scale of Punishments

One of the great achievements of the *philosophes* was their propaganda for the mitigation of the cruelties of criminal procedure as they had been practised in European society for centuries. Though his ideas were largely derived from Montesquieu, the North Italian, Cesare Bonesana, Marchese di Beccaria, a literary man and a professor, became one of the key figures in the movement to make the punishment fit the crime and to abolish torture. After his work won the imprimatur of Voltaire, who wrote a commentary on it, its success was phenomenal. From *An Essay on Crimes and Punishments* the Introduction and parts of the chapters "Of Estimating the Degree of Crimes" and "Of Torture" are presented. The book was published in 1764; the translation is an early one (London, 1767).

In every human society, there is an effort continually tending to confer on one part the height of power and happiness, and to reduce the other to the extreme of weakness, and misery. The intent of good laws is to oppose this effort, and to diffuse their influence, universally, and equally. But men generally abandon the care of their most important concerns to the uncertain prudence, and discretion of those, whose interest it is to reject the best, and wisest institutions; and it is not till they have been led into a thousand mistakes in matters, the most essential to their lives and liberties, and are weary of suffering, that they can be induced to apply a remedy to the evils, with which they are oppressed. It is then they begin to conceive, and acknowledge the most palpable truths, which, from their very simplicity, commonly escape vulgar minds, incapable of analysing objects, accustomed to receive impressions without distinction, and to be determined rather by the opinions of others, than by the result of their own examination.

If we look into history we shall find, that laws, which are, or ought to be, conventions between men in a state of freedom, have been, for the most part, the work of the passions of a few, or the consequences of a fortuitous, or temporary necessity; not dictated by a cool examiner of human nature, who knew how to collect in one point, the actions of a multitude, and had this only end in view, *the greatest happiness of the greatest number*. Happy are those few nations, who have not waited, till the slow succession of human vicissitudes, should, from the extremity of evil, produce a transition to good; but, by prudent laws, have facilitated the progress from one to the other! And how great are the obligations due from mankind to that philosopher, who from the obscurity of his closet, had the courage to scatter amongst the multitude, the seeds of useful truths, so long unfruitful!

The art of printing has diffused the knowledge of those philosophical truths, by which the relations between sovereigns and their subjects, and between nations, are discovered. By this knowledge, commerce is animated, and there has sprung up a spirit of emulation, and industry, worthy of rational beings. These are the produce of this enlightened age; but the cruelty of punishments, and the irregularity of proceedings in criminal cases, so principal a part of the legislation, and so much neglected throughout Europe, has hardly ever been called in question. Errors, accumulated through many centuries, have never yet been exposed by ascending to general principles; nor has the force of acknowledged truths been ever opposed to the unbounded licentiousness of ill-directed power, which has continually produced so many authorized examples of the most unfeeling barbarity. Surely, the groans of the weak, sacrificed to the cruel ignorance, and indolence of the powerful; the barbarous torments lavished, and multiplied with useless severity, for crimes either not proved, or in their nature impossible; the filth, and horrors of a prison, increased by the most cruel tormentor of the miserable, uncertainty, ought to have roused the attention of those, whose business is to direct the opinions of mankind.

The immortal *Montesquieu* has but slightly touched on this subject. Truth, which is eternally the same, has obliged me to follow the steps of that great man; but the studious part of mankind, for whom I write, will easily distinguish the superstructure from the foundation. I shall be happy, if, with him, I can obtain the secret thanks of the obscure, and peaceful disciples of reason, and philosophy, and excite that tender emotion, in which sensible minds sympathize with him, who pleads the cause of humanity.

Of the Proportion between Crimes and Punishments

It is not only the common interest of mankind, that crimes should not be committed, but that crimes of every kind should be less frequent, in proportion to the evil they produce to society. Therefore, the means made use of by the legislature to prevent crimes, should be more powerful, in proportion as they are destructive of the public safety and happiness, and as the inducements to commit them are stronger. Therefore there ought to be a fixed proportion between crimes and punishments.

It is impossible to prevent entirely all the disorders which the passions of mankind cause in society. These disorders increase in proportion to the number of people, and the opposition of private interests. If we consult history, we shall find them increasing, in every state, with the extent of dominion. In political arithmetic, it is necessary to substitute a calculation of probabilities, to mathematical exactness. That force, which continually impels us to our own private interest, like gravity, acts incessantly, unless it meets with an obstacle to oppose it. The effects of this force are the confused series of human actions. Punishments, which I would call political obstacles, prevent the fatal effects of private interest, without destroying the impelling cause, which is that sensibility inseparable from man. The legislator acts, in this case, like a skilful architect, who endeavours to counteract the force of gravity by combining the circumstances which may contribute to the strength of his edifice.

The necessity of uniting in society being granted, together with the conventions, which the opposite interests of individuals must necessarily require, a scale of crimes may be formed, of which the first degree should consist of those, which immediately tend to the dissolution of society, and the last, of the smallest possible injustice done to a private member of that society. Between these extremes will be comprehended, all actions contrary to the public good, which are called criminal, and which descend by insensible degrees, decreasing from the highest to the lowest. If mathematical calculation could be applied to the obscure and infinite combinations of human actions, there might be a corresponding scale of punishments, descending from the greatest to the least: but it will be sufficient that the wise legislator mark the principal divisions, without disturbing the order, lest to crimes of the *first* degree, be assigned punishments of the *last*. If there were an exact and universal scale of crimes and punishments, we should there have a common measure of the degree of liberty and slavery, humanity and cruelty of different nations.

Any action, which is not comprehended in the above-mentioned scale, will not be called a crime, or punished as such, except by those who have an interest in the denomination. The uncertainty of the extreme points of this scale, hath produced a system of morality which contradicts the laws; a multitude of laws that contradict each other; and many, which expose the best men to the severest punishments, rendering the ideas of *vice* and *virtue* vague, and fluctuating, and even their existence doubtful. Hence that fatal lethargy of political bodies, which terminates in their destruction.

Whoever reads, with a philosophic eye, the history of nations, and their laws, will generally find, that the ideas of virtue and vice, of a good or a bad citizen, change with the revolution of ages; not in proportion to the alteration of circumstances, and consequently conformable to the common good; but in proportion to the passions and errors by which the different law-givers were successively influenced. He will frequently observe, that the passions and vices of one age, are the foundation of the morality of the following; that violent passion, the offspring of fanatiscism and enthusiasm, being weakened by time, which reduces all the phenomena of the natural and moral world to an equality, become, by degrees, the prudence of the age, and an useful instrument in the hands of the powerful, or artful politician. Hence the uncertainty of our notions of honour and virtue; an uncertainty which will ever remain, because they change with the revolutions of time, and names survive the things they originally signified; they change with the boundaries of states, which are often the same both in physical and moral geography.

Pleasure and pain are the only springs of action in beings endowed with sensibility. Even amongst the motives which incite men to acts of religion, the invisible legislator has ordained rewards and punishments. From a partial distribution of these, will arise that contradiction, so little observed, because so common; I mean, that of punishing by the laws, the crimes which the laws have occasioned. If an equal punishment be ordained for two crimes that injure society in different degrees, there is nothing to deter men from committing the greater, as often as it is attended with greater advantage.

Of Estimating the Degree of Crimes

The foregoing reflections authorise me to assert, that crimes are only to be measured by the injury done to society.

They err, therefore, who imagine that a crime is greater, or less, according to the intention of the person by whom it is committed; for this will depend on the actual impression of objects on the senses, and on the previous disposition of the mind; both which will vary in different persons, and even in the same person at different times, according to the succession of ideas, passions, and circumstances. Upon that system, it would be necessary to form, not only a particular code for every individual, but a new penal law for every crime. Men, often with the best intention, do the greatest injury to society, and with the worst, do it the most essential services.

Others have estimated crimes rather by the dignity of the person offended, than by their consequences to society. If this were the true standard, the smallest irreverence to the divine Being ought to be punished with infinitely more severity, than the assassination of a monarch.

In short, others have imagined, that the greatness of the sin should aggravate the crime. But the fallacy of this opinion will appear on the slightest consideration of the relations between man and man, and between God and man. The relations between man and man, are relations of equality. Necessity alone hath produced, from the opposition of private passions and interests, the idea of public utility, which is the foundation of human justice. The other are relations of dependence, between an imperfect creature and his creator, the most perfect of beings, who has reserved to himself the sole right of being both lawgiver, and judge; for he alone can, without injustice, be, at the same time, both one and the other. If he hath decreed eternal punishments for those who disobey his will, shall an insect dare to put himself in the place of divine justice, or pretend to punish for the Almighty, who is himself all-sufficient; who cannot receive impressions of pleasure, or pain, and who alone, of all other beings, acts without being acted upon? The degree of sin depends on the malignity of the heart, which is impenetrable to finite beings. How then can the degree of sin serve as a standard to determine the degree of crimes? if that were admitted, men may punish when God pardons, and pardon when God condemns; and thus act in opposition to the supreme Being.

Of the Division of Crimes

We have proved, then, that crimes are to be estimated by *the injury done to society*. This is one of those palpable truths, which, though evident to the meanest capacity, yet, by a combination of circumstances, are only known to a few thinking men in every nation, and in every age. But opinions, worthy only of the despotism of Asia, and passions, armed with power and authority, have, generally by insensible and sometimes by violent impressions on the timid credulity of men, effaced those simple ideas, which perhaps constituted the first philosophy of infant society. Happily the philosophy of the present enlightened age seems again to conduct us to the same principles, and with that degree of certainty, which is obtained by a rational examination, and repeated experience.

Of Torture

The torture of a criminal, during the course of his trial, is a cruelty consecrated by custom in most nations. It is used with an intent either to make him confess his crime, or explain some contradictions, into which he had been led during his examination; or discover his accomplices; or for some kind of metaphysical and incomprehensible purgation of infamy; or, finally, in order to discover other crimes, of which he is not accused, but of which he may be guilty.

No man can be judged a criminal until he be found guilty; nor can society take from him the public protection, until it have been proved that he has violated the conditions on which it was granted. What right, then, but that of power, can authorize the punishment of a citizen, so long as there remains any doubt of his guilt? The dilemma is frequent. Either he is guilty, or not guilty. If guilty, he should only suffer the punishment ordained by the laws, and torture becomes useless, as his confession is unnecessary. If he be not guilty, you torture the innocent; for in the eye of the law, every man is innocent, whose crime has not been proved. Besides, it is confounding all relations, to expect that a man should be both the accuser and accused; and that pain should be the test of truth, as if truth resided in the muscles and fibres of a wretch in torture. By this method, the robust will escape, and the feeble be condemned. These are the inconveniences of this pretended test of truth, worthy only of a cannibal; and which the Romans, in many respects, barbarous, and whose savage virtue has been too much admired, reserved for the slaves alone.

What is the political intention of punishments? To terrify, and be an example to others. Is this intention answered, by thus privately torturing the guilty and the innocent? It is doubtless of importance, that no crime should remain unpunished; but it is useless to make a public example of the author of a crime hid in darkness. A crime already committed, and for which there can be no remedy, can only be punished by a political society, with an intention, that no hopes of impunity should induce others to commit the same. If it be true, that the number of those, who from fear or virtue respect the laws, is greater than of those by whom they are violated, the risk of torturing an innocent person is greater, as there is a greater probability, that, *caeteris paribus*, an individual hath observed, than that he hath infringed the laws.

There is another ridiculous motive for torture, namely, *to purge a man from infamy.* Ought such an abuse to be tolerated in the eighteenth century? Can pain, which is a sensation, have any connexion with a moral sentiment, a matter of opinion? Perhaps the rack may be considered as a refiner's furnace, the unerring light of revelation; and in the times of tractable ignorance, having no other, they naturally had recourse to it on every occasion, making the most remote and absurd applications. Moreover, infamy is a sentiment regulated neither by the laws nor by reason, but entirely by opinion. But torture renders the victim infamous, and therefore cannot take infamy away.

Another intention of torture is, to oblige the supposed criminal to reconcile the contradictions into which he may have fallen, during his examination; as if the dread of punishment, the uncertainty of his fate, the solemnity of the court, the majesty of the judge, and the ignorance of the accused, were not abundantly sufficient to account for contradictions, which are so common to men, even in a state of tranquility; and which must necessarily be multiplied by the perturbation of the mind of a man, entirely engaged in the thoughts of saving himself from imminent danger.

This infamous test of truth is a remaining monument of that antient and savage legislation, in which trials by fire, by boiling water, or the uncertainty of combats, were called *Judgments of God;* as if the links of that eternal chain, whose beginning is in the breast of the first cause of all things, could ever be disunited by the institutions of men. The only difference between torture, and trials by fire and boiling water, is, that the event of the first depends on the will of the accused; and of the second, on a fact entirely physical and external: but this difference is apparent only, not real. A man on the rack, in the convulsions of torture, has it as little in his power to declare the truth, as in former times, to prevent without fraud the effects of fire or of boiling water.

Every act of the will is invariably in proportion to the force of the impression on our senses. The impression of pain, then, may increase to such a degree, that occupying the mind entirely, it will compell the sufferer to use the shortest method of freeing himself from torment. His answer, therefore, will be an effect, as necessary as that of fire or boiling water; and he will accuse himself of crimes of which he is innocent. So that the very means employed to distinguish the innocent from the guilty, will most effectually destroy all difference between them.

It would be superfluous to confirm these reflections by examples of innocent persons, who, from the agony of torture, have confessed themselves guilty: innumerable instances may be found in all nations, and in every age. How amazing, that mankind have always neglected to draw the natural conclusion! Lives there a man who, if he have carried his thoughts ever so little beyond the necessities of life, when he reflects on such cruelty, is not tempted to fly from society, and return to his natural state of independence?

5. Mercier: The Execution of a Criminal

Louis Sébastien Mercier's *Memoirs of the Year Two Thousand Five Hundred* set a new style in Utopian thought when he depicted an ideal state at a future date instead of locating his perfect society on some distant island as Thomas More had done. We include this description of an execution as an example of the *philosophes'* concept of justice, purified of all feelings of vengeance. The laws have been "internalized" and the guilty man seeks his own death. The original appeared in French in 1771 and was translated into English by W. Hooper that same year. This passage is from the American edition (Philadelphia, 1795).

The repeated mournful sounds of a dreadful clarion suddenly struck my ear, and seemed to murmur to the air the names of misery and death; the drums of the city guard went slowly round, beating the alarm; and these ominous sounds, repeated by the mind, filled it with a profound horror. I saw the citizens come forth wth doleful aspects; each one addressed his neighbour, and lifting his eyes to heaven, wept, and showed all the tokens of the most piercing grief. I asked one of them, why tolled the funeral bells, and what accident had happened?

"One that is most terrible," he replied, with a groan. "Justice this day is forced to condemn a citizen to lose his life, of which he has rendered himself unworthy, by embruing his murdering hands in his brother's blood. More than thirty years have passed since the sun beheld a crime like this. Before the day is finished, he must expire. O, what tears have I shed for the fury that drove him to such a blind vengeance! Have you heard the particulars of the crime that was committed the night before the last? O grief! is it not enough that we have lost one worthy citizen; but must another suffer death?"—He sighed bitterly.—"Hear, hear the story

148

of that direful event, which has spread over us an universal lamentation.

"One of our fellow-citizens, of a fiery disposition, from his birth remarkable for passion, though otherwise a man of merit, was on the point of being married to a young woman whom he loved to distraction. Her temper was as gentle as that of her lover was impetuous; she flattered herself, however, with being able to soften his manners; but the many sallies of wrath that escaped him, notwithstanding all his care to conceal them, made her tremble for the direful consequences that might proceed from a union with a man of his violent temper. Every woman, by our law, is absolute mistress of her person; she therefore determined, from a fear of being miserable, to marry another, who was of a character more comformable to her own. The torch of these nuptials set fire to the rage of an implacable heart, which in the tenderest years had never known moderation. He gave many private challenges to his happy rival, who despised them; for he knew there was more bravery in disdaining an insult, and in stifling a resentment, than in yielding to the impulse of passion, in a manner that both our laws and reason proscribe. The enraged man, listening to nothing but jealousy, rencountered the other, the day before yesterday, in a private path without the city, and on his refusing again to combat with him, he seized a branch of a tree, and laid him dead at his feet. After this horrid act, the inhuman wretch dared to come amongst us; but his crime was already engraved on his front; we no sooner saw him, than we discovered that he was criminal, though then ignorant of the nature of his offence. But soon we saw several citizens; their cheeks wet with tears, who bore, with solemn steps, to the foot of the throne of justice, the bloody corpse that cried for vengeance.

"At the age of fourteen, they read to us the laws of our country. Every one is obliged to write them with his own hand, and to make oath that he will observe them. These laws command us to inform the police of all those infractions that offend against the order of society; but they intend those matters only that cause a real detriment. We renew this sacred oath every ten years; and without being busy informers, religiously watch over the preservation of our venerable laws.

"Yesterday they published the monitory, which is an act entirely civil. Whoever should delay to declare what he knew would be branded with infamy. By this means it is that homicide is soon discovered. None but a villain, for a long time familiarized with guilt, can coolly deny the crime he has just committed; and of this sort of monsters our nation is purged; they no longer terrify us, but in the histories of past ages.

"Obey, with me, the voice of justice, that calls all the people to be witness of its awful decrees. It is the day of its triumph; and, fatal as it is, we receive it with applause. You will not see a wretch who has been plunged for six months in a dungeon, his eyes dazzled by the light of the sun, his bones broken by a previous and secret punishment more horrible than that he is going to suffer, advance with hideous and dying looks, towards a scaffold erected in an obscure nook. In your time, the criminal, judged in the secrecy of a prison, was sometimes broke on the wheel in the silence of the night, at the door of some sleeping citizen; who waking with terror at the cries of the excruciated wretch, was uncertain whether he was suffering under the iron bar of an executioner, or the sword of an assassin. We have none of those tortures that are shocking to nature; we have a regard to humanity even with them who have offended against it. In your age, they seemed not to be content with merely putting a man to death, so little effect the tragic scenes had upon you, all horrible as they were, and multiplied in cold blood. The guilty, far from being dragged along in a manner that is disgraceful to justice, is not even fettered. Alas! why should he be loaded with chains, when he freely delivers himself up to death? Justice has full power to condemn him to death, but not to charge him with marks of slavery. You will see him walk freely in the midst of some soldiers, who surround him merely to keep off the multitude. We have no fear that he will a second time disgrace himself by endeavouring to fly from the terrible voice that accuses him. Whither should he fly? What country, what people would receive among them an assassin? and how could he ever efface that horrid mark which the hand of the Divinity imprints on the front of a murderer; the tempest of remorse is there painted in glaring characters; and the eye accustomed to the aspect of virtue will easily distinguish the physiognomy of guilt. How, in short, can he ever be free who feels the immense weight that presses upon his heart?"

We arrived at a spacious place that surrounded the palace of justice. Along the front of the hall of audience there ran a large flight of steps. It was on this kind of amphitheatre that the senate assembled on public affairs, in the sight of the people; it was under their inspection that it chose to transact the most important affairs of the nation; the numerous body of citizens there assembled inspired them with sentiments worthy of the august concerns committed to their care. The death of a citizen was a calamity to the state. The judges failed not to give their sentence all that solemnity, all that importance it deserved. The order of advocates were on one side, constantly ready to plead for the innocent, but silent in the cause of the guilty. On the other side, the prelate, accompanied by the pastors, bare-headed, silently invoked the God of Mercy, and edified the people, spread in crowds all over the place.

The criminal appeared; he was dressed in a bloody shirt; he beat his breast, and shewed all the marks of a sincere repentance. His visage, however, expressed nothing of that dreadful embarrassment so unbecoming a man, who ought to know how to die when necessity calls, and especially when he merits death. They made him pass by a sort of cage, where, they told me, the body of the murdered man was exposed. On his near approach, he was seized with such violent remorse, that they suffered him to retire. He approached the judges, and put one knee to the ground, to kiss the sacred volume of the law. It was then opened to him, and they read, with a loud voice, the sentence relative to homicides; they placed the book before him, that he might read it; he then fell on his knees, and confessed his guilt. The head of the senate, mounting a platform that was prepared for him, read his condemnation with a strong and majestic voice. All the counsellors, as well as the advocates, who were standing, then sat down, by which they declared that no one of them would undertake his defence.

When the head of the senate had done reading, he deigned to stretch out his hand to the criminal, and raise him up; he then said, "Nothing now remains for you but to die with firmness, and obtain your pardon of God and of men. We do not hate you; we grieve for you, and your memory will not be held in detestation by us. Obey the law with cheerfulness, and revere its salutary rigour. Our tears bear witness that affection will take place in our hearts, when justice shall have accomplished her fatal decrees. Death is less dreadful than ignominy. Submit to the one, to avoid the other. It is still in your power to choose. If you will live, you may; but in must be in disgrace, and loaded with our indignation. You will behold the sun constantly upbraiding you with having deprived your fellow-being of his genial and brilliant rays; to you they will be hateful, as they will only discover those disdainful looks with which all men regard an assassin. You will bear about with you every where the load of your remorse, and the eternal shame of having refused to submit to that just law which has condemned you. Do justice to society and condemn yourself."

The criminal bowed his head; by which he declared that he judged himself deserving of death. He immediately prepared to submit with constancy and with that resignation which, in our last moments, is so highly becoming of humanity. He was no longer regarded as guilty; the body of pastors surrounded him; the prelate taking off the bloody shirt, clothed him in a white vestment, which was the token of his reconciliation with mankind, and gave him the kiss of peace. His friends and relations crowded to embrace him; he appeared satisfied by receiving their caresses, and by being vested with that garment which was a proof of the pardon he received from his country. Those testimonies of friendship took from him the horrors of approaching death. The prelate, advancing towards the people, seized that moment to make a nervous and pathetic discourse on the danger of passion; it was so eloquent, so just and affecting, that every heart was filled with admiration and terror. Each one resolved to watch carefully over his temper and stifle those seeds of resentment, which increase in a manner unknown to ourselves, and soon produce the most unbridled passions.

During this interval, a deputy from the senate bore the sentence of death to the monarch, that he might sign it with his own hand; for no one could be put to death without his own consent, as in him resided the power of the sword. That good father would gladly have spared the life of the criminal; but, in that moment he sacrificed the earnest desire of his heart to the necessity of an exemplary justice.

The deputy returned. Then again the bells of the city began their funeral tolls, the drums repeated their mournful march, and those deploring sounds meeting in the air with the groans of the numerous people one would have thought that the city was on the brink of an universal destruction. The friends and relations of the unfortunate man going to meet his death, gave him the last embrace; the prelate invoked with a loud voice, the forgiveness of the Supreme Being, and the vaulted roof of heaven resounded with the supplications of the whole people, who cried, with one mighty voice, "*O Almighty God, receive his soul! O God of Mercy, forgive him, even as we forgive him!*"

They conducted him, with slow steps, to the cage I have mentioned, still surrounded by his friends. Six fusileers, their faces covered with crape, advanced; the head of the senate gave the signal, by holding up the book of the law; they fired and the soul disappeared. They took up the dead body. His crime being fully expiated by his punishment, he was again received into the class of citizens; his name, that had been effaced, was inscribed again in the public register, with the names of those who had died the same day. This people had not the cruelty to pursue the memory of a man even to his tomb; and to reflect on a whole innocent family the crime of an individual; they did not find pleasure in dishonouring, without a cause, useful citizens, and make men miserable, for the satisfaction of making them humble. His body was carried to be burned without the city, with his fellow-citizens, who, the preceding day, had paid the inevitable debt to nature; his relations had no other grief to encounter than that which arose from the loss of a friend. The same evening, a place of trust and honour becoming vacant, the king conferred it on the brother of the criminal; and every one applauded a choice that was dictated by equity and beneficence.

With a heart full of tenderness and commiseration, I said, O, how is humanity respected among you! The death of a citizen is the cause of universal mourning to his country.—"It is because our laws," they replied, "are wise and humane; they are calculated more for reformation than for chastisement; the way to intimidate vice is not to render punishment common, but formidable; it is our study to prevent crimes; we send the refractory to places of solitude, where they are attended by those who endeavour to bring them to repentance, who operate by degrees on their hardened hearts, and gradually display the refined charms of virtue, to whose attractions the most depraved of mortals are not insensible. Does the physician at the first attack of a violent fever abandon his patient? Why, therefore, should we desert the guilty who may yet be recovered? There are few hearts so corrupted, as not to be restored by perseverance; and a little blood properly poured forth, cements our tranquillity and our happiness.

"Your penal laws were all made in favour of the rich; all fell on the head of the poor; gold was become the god of nations; edicts and gibbets surrounded all possessions; and tyranny, with sword in hand, bartered the days, the sweat and blood of the unfortunate; it made no distinction in chastisements, and thereby taught the people to make none in crimes; it punished the least offence as the most infamous villainy. What was the consequence? The multiplying of laws multiplied crimes, and the offenders became as inhuman as their judges. Legislation, when it attempted to unite the members of society, drew the bands so tight as to throw it into convulsions; and, instead of maintaining, destroyed the connections; mournful humanity sent forth the cry of grief, and saw too late, that the tortures of the executioner never inspire virtue."

Part Five

✸ THE FUTURE PROSPECT

1. Gibbon: Lessons of History

The Decline and Fall of the Roman Empire by Edward Gibbon
is the greatest historical masterpiece of the Enlightenment. In
a section of the third volume entitled "General Observations
on the Fall of the Roman Empire in the West" (the work appeared in six volumes from 1776 through 1788), Gibbon com-
bines a cautious though specific condemnation of Christianity
for the final breakdown with a belief in the relative immunity
of his own society from a similar fate. Progress in wealth, happiness, and knowledge is affirmed—though faith in moral
progress, in "virtue," is still somewhat circumspect.

As the happiness of a *future* life is the great object of
religion, we may hear without surprise or scandal, that the introduction, or at least the abuse of Christianity, had some influence on
the decline and fall of the Roman empire. The clergy successfully
preached the doctrines of patience and pusillanimity; the active
virtues of society were discouraged; and the last remains of military
spirit were buried in the cloister: a large portion of public and
private wealth was consecrated to the specious demands of charity
and devotion; and the soldiers' pay was lavished on the useless
multitudes of both sexes, who could only plead the merits of ab-
stinence and chastity. Faith, zeal, curiosity, and the more earthly
passions of malice and ambition, kindled the flame of theological

discord; the church, and even the state, were distracted by religious factions, whose conflicts were sometimes bloody, and always implacable; the attention of the emperors was diverted from camps to synods; the Roman world was oppressed by a new species of tyranny; and the persecuted sects became the secret enemies of their country. Yet party-spirit, however pernicious or absurd, is a principle of union as well as of dissension. The bishops, from eighteen hundred pulpits, inculcated the duty of passive obedience to a lawful and orthodox sovereign; their frequent assemblies, and perpetual correspondence, maintained the communion of distant churches; and the benevolent temper of the Gospel was strengthened, though confined, by the spiritual alliance of the Catholics. The sacred indolence of the monks was devoutly embraced by a servile and effeminate age; but if superstition had not afforded a decent retreat, the same vices would have tempted the unworthy Romans to desert, from baser motives, the standard of the republic. Religious precepts are easily obeyed, which indulge and sanctify the natural inclinations of their votaries; but the pure and genuine influence of Christianity may be traced in its beneficial, though imperfect, effects on the Barbarian proselytes of the North. If the decline of the Roman empire was hastened by the conversion of Constantine, his victorious religion broke the violence of the fall, and mollified the ferocious temper of the conquerors.

This awful revolution may be usefully applied to the instruction of the present age. It is the duty of a patriot to prefer and promote the exclusive interest and glory of his native country: but a philosopher may be permitted to enlarge his views, and to consider Europe as one great republic, whose various inhabitants have attained almost the same level of politeness and cultivation. The balance of power will continue to fluctuate, and the prosperity of our own, or the neighbouring kingdoms, may be alternately exalted or depressed; but these partial events cannot essentially injure our general state of happiness, the system of arts, and laws, and manners, which so advantageously distinguish, above the rest of mankind, the Europeans and their colonies. The savage nations of the globe are the common enemies of civilised society; and we may inquire, with anxious curiosity, whether Europe is still threatened with a repetition of those calamities, which formerly oppressed the arms and institutions of Rome. Perhaps the same reflections will illustrate the fall of that mighty empire, and explain the probable causes of our actual security.

The Romans were ignorant of the extent of their danger, and the number of their enemies. Beyond the Rhine and Danube, the Northern countries of Europe and Asia were filled with innumerable tribes of hunters and shepherds, poor, voracious, and turbulent; bold in arms, and impatient to ravish the fruits of industry. The Barbarian world was agitated by the rapid impulse of war; and the peace of Gaul or Italy was shaken by the distant revolutions of China. The Huns, who fled before a victorious enemy, directed their march towards the West; and the torrent was swelled by the gradual accession of captives and allies. The flying tribes who yielded to the Huns assumed in *their* turn the spirit of conquest; the endless column of Barbarians pressed on the Roman empire with accumulated weight; and, if the foremost were destroyed, the vacant space was instantly replenished by new assailants. Such formidable emigrations can no longer issue from the North; and the long repose, which has been imputed to the decrease of population, is the happy consequence of the progress of arts and agriculture. Instead of some rude villages, thinly scattered among its woods and morasses, Germany now produces a list of two thousand three hundred walled towns: the Christian kingdoms of Denmark, Sweden, and Poland, have been successively established; and the Hanse merchants, with the Teutonic knights, have extended their colonies along the coast of the Baltic, as far as the Gulf of Finland. From the Gulf of Finland to the Eastern Ocean, Russia now assumes the form of a powerful and civilised empire. The plough, the loom, and the forge, are introduced on the banks of the Volga, the Oby, and the Lena; and the fiercest of the Tartar hordes have been taught to tremble and obey. The reign of independent Barbarism is now contracted to a narrow span; and the remnant of Calmucks or Uzbecks, whose forces may be almost numbered, cannot seriously excite the apprehensions of the great republic of Europe. Yet this apparent security should not tempt us to forget, that new enemies, and unknown dangers, may *possibly* arise from some obscure people, scarcely visible in the map of the world. The Arabs or Saracens, who spread their conquests from India to Spain, had languished in poverty and contempt, till Mahomet breathed into those savage bodies the soul of enthusiasm.

The empire of Rome was firmly established by the singular and perfect coalition of its members. The subject nations, resigning the hope, and even the wish, of independence, embraced the character of Roman citizens; and the provinces of the West were reluctantly torn by the Barbarians from the bosom of their mother country. But this union was purchased by the loss of national freedom and military spirit; and the servile provinces, destitute of life and motion, expected their safety from the mercenary troops and governors, who were directed by the orders of a distant court. The happiness of an hundred millions depended on the personal merit of one or two men, perhaps children, whose minds were corrupted by education, luxury, and despotic power. The deepest wounds were inflicted on the empire during the minorities of the sons and grandsons of Theodosius; and, after those incapable princes seemed to attain the age of manhood, they abandoned the church to the bishops, the state to the eunuchs, and the provinces to the Barbarians. Europe is now divided into twelve powerful, though unequal kingdoms, three respectable commonwealths, and a variety of smaller, though independent, states: the chances of royal and ministerial talents are multiplied, at least, with the number of its rulers; and a Julian, or Semiramis, may reign in the North, while Arcadius and Honorius again slumber on the thrones of the South. The abuses of tyranny are restrained by the mutual influence of fear and shame; republics have acquired order and stability; monarchies have imbibed the principles of freedom, or, at least, of moderation; and some sense of honour and justice is introduced into the most defective constitutions by the general manners of the times. In peace, the progress of knowledge and industry is accelerated by the emulation of so many active rivals: in war, the European forces are exercised by temperate and undecisive contests. If a savage conqueror should issue from the deserts of Tartary, he must repeatedly vanquish the robust peasants of Russia, the numerous armies of Germany, the gallant nobles of France, and the intrepid freemen of Britain; who, perhaps, might confederate for their common defence. Should the victorious Barbarians carry slavery and desolation as far as the Atlantic Ocean, ten thousand vessels would transport beyond their pursuit the remains of civilised society; and Europe would revive and flourish in the American world, which is already filled with her colonies and institutions.

Cold, poverty, and a life of danger and fatigue, fortify the strength and courage of Barbarians. In every age they have oppressed the polite and peaceful nations of China, India, and Persia, who neglected, and still neglect, to counterbalance these natural powers by the resources of military art. The warlike states of antiquity, Greece, Macedonia, and Rome, educated a race of soldiers; exercised their bodies, disciplined their courage, multiplied their forces by regular evolutions, and converted the iron, which they possessed, into strong and serviceable weapons. But this superiority insensibly declined with their laws and manners; and the feeble policy of Constantine and his successors armed and instructed, for the ruin of the empire, the rude valour of the Barbarian mercenaries. The military art has been changed by the invention of gunpowder; which enables man to command the two most powerful agents of nature, air and fire. Mathematics, chemistry, mechanics, architecture, have been applied to the service of war; and the adverse parties oppose to each other the most elaborate modes of attack and of defence. Historians may indignantly observe, that the preparations of a siege would found and maintain a flourishing colony; yet we cannot be displeased, that the subversion of a city should be a work of cost and difficulty; or that an industrious people should be protected by those arts, which survive and supply the decay of military virtue. Cannon and fortifications now form an impregnable barrier against the Tartar horse; and Europe is secure from any future irruption of Barbarians; since, before they can conquer, they must cease to be barbarous. Their gradual advances in the science of war would always be accompanied, as we may learn from the example of Russia, with a proportionable improvement in the arts of peace and civil policy; and they themselves must deserve a place among the polished nations whom they subdue.

Should these speculations be found doubtful or fallacious, there still remains a more humble source of comfort and hope. The discoveries of ancient and modern navigators, and the domestic history, or tradition, of the most enlightened nations, represent the *human savage,* naked both in mind and body, and destitute of laws, of arts, of ideas, and almost of language. From this abject condition, perhaps the primitive and universal state of man, he has gradually arisen to command the animals, to fertilise the earth, to traverse the ocean, and to measure the heavens. His progress in the improvement and exercise of his mental and corporeal faculties has been irregular and various; infinitely slow in the beginning, and increasing by degrees with redoubled velocity: ages of laborious ascent have been followed by a moment of rapid downfall; and the several climates of the globe have felt the vicissitudes of light and darkness. Yet the experience of four thousand years should enlarge our hopes, and diminish our apprehensions: we cannot determine to what height the human species may aspire in their advances towards perfection; but it may safely be presumed, that no people, unless the face of nature is changed, will relapse into their original barbarism. The improvements of society may be viewed under a threefold aspect. 1. The poet or philosopher illustrates his age and country by the efforts of a *single* mind; but these superior powers of reason or fancy are rare and spontaneous productions; and the genius of Homer, or Cicero, or Newton, would excite less admiration, if they could be created by the will of a prince, or the lessons of a preceptor. 2. The benefits of law and policy, of trade and manufactures, of arts and sciences, are more solid and permanent; and *many* individuals may be qualified, by education and discipline, to promote, in their respective stations, the interest of the community. But this general order is the effect of skill and labour; and the complex machinery may be decayed by time, or injured by violence. 3. Fortunately for mankind, the more useful, or, at least, more necessary arts, can be performed without superior talents, or national subordination; without the powers of *one,* or the union of *many.* Each village, each family, each individual, must always possess both ability and inclination, to perpetuate the use of fire and of metals; the propagation and service of domestic animals; the methods of hunting and fishing; the rudiments of navigation; the imperfect cultivation of corn, or other nutritive grain; and the simple practice of the mechanic trades. Private genius and public industry may be extirpated; but these hardy plants survive the tempest, and strike an everlasting root into the most unfavourable soil. The splendid days of Augustus and Trajan were eclipsed by a cloud of ignorance; and the Barbarians subverted the laws and palaces of Rome. But the scythe, the invention or emblem of Saturn, still continued annually to mow the harvests of Italy; and the human feasts of the Læstrigons have never been renewed on the coast of Campania.

Since the first discovery of the arts, war, commerce, and religious zeal have diffused, among the savages of the Old and New World, these inestimable gifts: they have been successively propagated; they can never be lost. We may therefore acquiesce in the pleasing conclusion, that every age of the world has increased, and still increases, the real wealth, the happiness, the knowledge, and perhaps the virtue, of the human race.

2. Herder: The Tenacity of National Genius

The uniqueness of each culture and its right to an independent existence is one of the central moral themes of Johann Gottfried von Herder's philosophy of history. He developed the concept of *Volk* genius with an intensity of passion that made his work the Bible of European cultural nationalism, particularly in Central and Eastern Europe. The original German edition of *Outlines of a Philosophy of the History of Man* was published in Riga from 1784 to 1791. We quote from the English translation by Thomas Churchill (London, 1800).

The one Species of Man has naturalized itself in every Climate upon Earth

Observe yon locusts of the Earth, the kalmuc and mungal: they are fitted for no region but their own hills and mountains. The light rider flies on his little horse over immense tracts of the desert; he knows how to invigorate his fainting courser, and by opening a vein in his neck, to restore his own powers, when *He* sinks with fatigue. No rain falls on many parts of these regions, which are refreshed solely by the dew, while inexhaustible fertility clothes the earth with continually renovated verdure. Throughout many extensive tracts no tree is to be seen, no spring of fresh water to be discovered. Here these wild tribes, yet preserving good order among themselves, wander about among the luxuriant grass, and pasture their herds: the horses, their associates, know their voices, and live like them in peace. With thoughtless indifference sits the indolent kalmuc, contemplating the undisturbed serenity of his sky, while his ear catches every sound, that pervades the desert his eye is unable to scan. In every other region of the Earth the mungal has either degenerated or improved: in his own

162

country he is what he was thousands of years ago, and such will he continue, as long as it remains unaltered by Nature or by art.

The arab of the desert belongs to it, as much as his noble horse, and his patient, indefatigable camel. As the mungal wanders over his heights, and among his hills, so wanders the better-formed bedouin over his extensive asiatic-african deserts; also a nomade, but a nomade of *his own* region. With this his simple clothing, his maxims of life, his manners, and his character, are in unison; and, after the lapse of thousands of years, his tent still preserves the wisdom of his forefathers. A lover of liberty, he despises wealth and pleasure, is fleet in the course, a dextrous manager of his horse, of whom he is as careful as of himself, and equally dextrous in handling the javelin. His figure is lean and muscular, his complexion brown; his bones strong. He is indefatigable in supporting labour, bold and enterprizing, faithful to his word, hospitable and magnanimous, and, connected with his fellows by the desert, he makes one common cause with all. From the dangers of his mode of life he has imbibed wariness and shy mistrust; from his solitary abode, the feelings of revenge, friendship, enthusiasm, and pride. Wherever an arab is found, on the Nile or the Euphrates, on Libanus or in Senegal, nay even in Zanguebar or the islands of the indian ocean, if a foreign climate have not by length of time changed him into a colonist, he will display his original arabian character.

The californian, on the verge of the earth, in his barren country, exposed as he is to want, and amid the vicissitudes of his climate, complains not of heat or cold, eludes the force of hunger, though with the utmost difficulty, and enjoys happiness in his native land. "God alone can tell," says a missionary, "how many thousand miles a californian, that has attained the age of eighty, must have wandered over before he finds a grave. Many of them change their quarters perhaps a hundred times in a year, sleeping scarcely three nights together on the same spot, or in the same region. They lie down wherever night overtakes them, without paying the least regard to the filthiness of the soil, or endeavouring to secure themselves from noxious vermin. Their dark brown skin serves them instead of coat and cloak. Their furniture consists of a bow and arrows, a stone for a knife, a bone or sharp stakes to dig up roots, the shell of a tortoise for a cradle, a gut or a bladder to carry water, and, if they be peculiarly fortunate, a pouch made of the fibres of the aloe, somewhat in the fashion of a net, to contain their utensils and provision. They feed on roots, and all sorts of small seeds, even those of grass, which they collect with great labour; nay, when pressed by want, they pick them out of their own dung. Every thing that can be called flesh, or barely resembles it, even to bats, grubs, and worms, is to be reckoned among the dainties, on which they feast; and the leaves of certain shrubs, with their young shoots, leather, and spungy bones, are not excluded from their list of provision, when urged by hunger. Yet these poor creatures are healthy: they live to a great age, and are strong; so that it is uncommon to see a man grayheaded, and never but at a late period. They are always cheerful; for ever jesting and laughing; well made, straight, and active; they can lift stones and other things from the ground with their two foremost toes; they walk as erect as a dart to the extreme of old age; and the children go alone before they are a year old. When weary of talking, they lie down and sleep, till awakened by hunger, or the desire of eating: and as soon as they are awake, the laugh, the talk, and the jest, recommence. Thus they go on, till worn out by old age, when they meet death with calm indifference. The inhabitant of Europe," continues the missionary, "may envy the happiness of the californian: but for this the native of California is indebted solely to his perfect indifference whether he possess much or little in this world, and his absolute resignation to the will of God in all the occurrences of life."

In this manner I might go on, and exhibit climatic pictures of several nations, inhabiting the most different regions, from Kamtschatka to Tierra del Fuego: but why should I give these brief sketches, since every traveller, who sees with accuracy, or feels as a man, gives the shade of the climate to every little stroke of his delineations? In India, the grand resort of commercial nations, the arab and the chinese, the turk and the persian, the christian and the jew, the negro and the malay, the japanese and the gentoo, are clearly distinguishable: thus every one bears the characters of his country and way of life on the most distant shores. The ancient allegorical tradition says, that Adam was formed out of the dust of all the four quarters of the Globe, and animated by the powers and spirits of the whole Earth. Wherever his children have bent their course, and fixed their abode, in the lapse of ages, there they have taken root as trees, and produced leaves and fruit adapted to the climate. Hence let us deduce a few consequences, which seem to explain to us many things, that might otherwise be deemed striking singularities in the history of man.

In the first place it is obvious why all sensual people, fashioned to their country, are so much attached to the soil, and so inseparable from it. The constitution of their body, their way of life, the pleasures and occupations to which they have been accustomed from their infancy, and the whole circle of their ideas, are climatic. Deprive them of their country, you deprive them of every thing.

"It has been remarked," says Cranz, "of the six greenlanders, who were brought over to Denmark, that, notwithstanding all the friendly treatment they received, and the abundance of stockfish and train-oil, with which they were supplied, their eyes were often turned toward the north and their native country, with melancholy looks and piteous sighs; and at length they attempted to make their escape in their canoe. A strong gale having driven them on the coast of Scania, they were brought back to Copenhagen, when two of them died of grief. Two of the others again ran away, and only one of them was retaken, who wept bitterly whenever he saw a child in its mother's arms; whence it was inferred, that he had a wife and children, for no one was able to converse with him, or prepare him for baptism. The last two lived ten or twelve years in Denmark, and were employed in the pearl-fishery at Coldingen, but were so hard-worked in winter, that one of them died. The other, again attempting to escape, was retaken thirty or forty leagues from land, when he too died of grief."

No words can express the sorrow and despair of a bought or stolen negro slave, when he leaves his native shore, never more to behold it while he has breath. "Great care must be taken," says Roemer, "that the slaves do not get hold of a knife, either in the fort, or aboard the ship. To keep them in good humour on their passage to the West Indies requires the utmost exertion. For this purpose violins are provided, with fifes and drums; they are permitted to dance; and they are assured, that they are going to a pleasant country, where they may have as many wives as they please, and plenty of good food. Yet many deplorable instances have been known of their falling upon the crew, murdering them, and letting the ship drive ashore." But how many more deplorable instances have been known of these poor stolen wretches destroying themselves in despair! Sparmann informs us, from the mouth of a slavedealer, that at night they are seized with a kind of frenzy, which prompts them to commit murder, either on themselves or others; "for the painful recollection of the irreparable loss of their country and their freedom commonly awakes by night, when the bustle of the day ceases to engage their attention." And what right have you, monsters! even to approach the country of these unfortunates, much less to tear them from it by stealth, fraud, and cruelty? For ages this quarter of the Globe has been theirs, and they belong to it: their forefathers purchased it at a dear rate, at the price of the negro form and complexion. In fashioning them the african sun has adopted them as it's children, and impressed on them it's own seal: wherever you convey them, this brands you as robbers, as stealers of men.

Concluding Remarks on the Opposition between Genesis and Climate

If I mistake not, the hints, that have been given, may be considered as the commencement of the line, that marks this opposition. No man will expect, for instance, that the rose should become a lilly, the dog a wolf, in a foreign climate: for Nature has drawn determinate lines round her species, and permits a creature rather to disappear, than essentially deface or falsify it's figure. But, that the rose can admit of variation, that the dog can acquire something wolfish, is conformable to experience: yet here the variation is producible only by slow or speedy violence done to the resisting organic powers. Thus both the contending principles act with great force, yet each in it's own way. Climate is a chaos of causes, very dissimilar to each other, and in consequence acting slowly and in various ways, till at length they penetrate to the internal parts, and change them by habit, and by the genetic power itself: this resists long, forcibly, uniformly, and like itself; but as it is not independent of external affections, it also must accommodate itself to them in length of time.

1. *Too sudden, too precipitate transitions to an opposite hemisphere and climate are seldom salutary to a nation;* for Nature has not established her boundaries between remote lands in vain. The history of conquests, as well as of commercial companies, and especially that of missions, afford a melancholy, and in some respects a laughable picture, if we delineate this subject and it's consequences with impartiality, even from the narrations of the parties themselves. We shudder with abhorrence when we read the accounts of many european nations, who, sunk in the most dissolute voluptuousness and insensible pride, have degenerated both in body and mind, and no longer possess any capacity for enjoyment and compassion. They are fullblown bladders in human shape, lost to every noble and active pleasure, and in whose veins lurks avenging death. If to these we add the wretches, to whom both the Indies have proved insatiate graves; if we read the histories of the diseases of foreign climates, given by english, french, and dutch physicians; and if we then turn our eyes to the pious missionaries, who have not been so ready to quit the garb of their order, and their european mode of life; what instructive inferences press upon us, which alas! belong to the history of man!

2. *Even the european industry of less debauched colonies in other quarters of the Globe is not always able to avert the effect of climate.* It is observed by Kalm, that the europeans in North-America arrive earlier at the age of puberty, but at the same time sooner grow old and die, than in their native country. "It is nothing uncommon," says he, "to find little children answer questions put to them with astonishing readiness and vivacity, and yet not attain the age of europeans. Eighty or ninety years are seldom reached by one born in America of european parents, though the aborigines frequently live much longer: and the natives of Europe commonly live much longer in America, than such of their children as are born in that country. The women sooner cease child-bearing, some as early as the age of thirty: and it is generally observed, that the offspring of the european colonists lose their teeth soon and prematurely, while the americans retain their teeth white and sound to the end of their lives." This passage has been improperly quoted

as a proof of the unhealthiness of America with respect to her own children: but it is to foreigners only that she is a stepmother, who, as Kalm observes, dwell in her bosom with different constitutions and manners.

3. *Let it not be imagined, that human art can with despotic power convert at once a foreign region into another Europe,* by cutting down it's forests, and cultivating it's soil: for it's whole living creation is conformable to it, and this is not to be changed at discretion. Even Kalm informs us, from the mouths of american swedes, that the speedy destruction of the woods, and cultivation of the land, not only lessened the number of edible birds, which were found in innumerable multitudes in the forests and on the waters, and of fishes with which the brooks and rivers swarmed, and diminished the lakes, streams, rivulets, springs, rains, thick long grass of the woods, &c.; but seemed to affect the health and longevity of the inhabitants, and influence the seasons. "The americans," says he, "who frequently lived a hundred years and upwards before the arrival of the europeans, now often attain scarcely half the age of their forefathers: and this, it is probable, we must not ascribe solely to the destructive use of spirits, and an alteration in their way of life, but likewise to the loss of so many odoriferous herbs, and salutary plants, which every morning and evening perfumed the air, as if the country had been a flower garden. The winter was then more seasonable, cold, healthy, and constant: now the spring commences later, and, like the other seasons, is more variable and irregular." This is the account given by Kalm; and however local we may consider it, still it shows, that Nature loves not too speedy, too violent a change, even in the best work, that man can perform, the cultivation of a country. May we not also attribute the debility of the civilized americans, as they are called, in Mexico, Peru, Paraguay, and Brasil, to this among other things, that we have changed their country and manner of living, without the power or the will of giving them an european nature? All the nations, that live in the woods, and after the manner of their forefathers, are strong and bold, live long, and renovate their vigour like their own trees: those on the cultivated land, deprived of shade and moisture, decline miserably; their souls are left behind in the

woods. Read, as an example, the affecting history of a simple flourishing family, drawn from it's wilds by Dobritzhofer. Both the mother and daughter soon died; and both in dreams continued to call on their son and brother left behind, till death closed his eyes without the aid of disease. This alone renders it comprehensible, how nations, that once were valiant, active, and resolute, should in a short time sink into such a state of weakness, as the jesuits of Paraguay and travellers in Peru describe: a weakness of which we cannot read without sorrow. In the course of ages this subjugation of Nature may have it's good effects in particular places; though I doubt this, if it were generally practicable: but for the first races, both of the civilizers and civilized, it appears to have none; for Nature is every where a living whole, and will be gently followed and improved, not mastered by force. Nothing has been made of any of the savages, who have been suddenly brought into the throng of an european city: from the splendid height, on which they were placed, they longed for their native plains, and for the most part returned inexpert and corrupted to their ancient way of life, which also they were now rendered incapable of enjoying. It is the same with the forcible alteration of savage climates by european hands.

O sons of Dedalus, emissaries of Fate, how many instruments are in your hands for conferring happiness on nations by humane and compassionate means! and how has a proud insolent love of gain led you almost every where into a different path! All new comers from a foreign land, who have submitted to naturalize themselves with the inhabitants, have not only enjoyed their love and friendship, but have ultimately found, that their mode of life was not altogether unsuitable to the climate: but how few such are there! how seldom does an european hear from the native of any country the praise, "he is a rational man like us!" And does not Nature revenge every insult offered her? Where are the conquests, the factories, the invasions, of former times, when distant foreign lands were visited by a different race, for the sake of devastation or plunder! The still breath of climate has dissipated or consumed them, and it was not difficult for the natives to give the finishing stroke to the rootless tree. The quiet plant, on the other hand, that has accommodated itself to the laws of Nature, has not only preserved it's own existence, but has beneficially diffused the seeds of cultivation through a new land. Future ages may decide, what benefit, or injury, our genius has conferred on other climates, and other climates on our genius.

3. Kant: Definitive Articles of Peace

Project for a Perpetual Peace was one of the last works published by Immanuel Kant and it fitted in with his belief in the inevitability of moral progress and the ethical perfection of man. In this essay he presented both preliminary and definitive articles of perpetual peace among states. Kant held that morality was indivisible: there could be no truly moral man within a state so long as that state sent its citizens into battle against fellow human beings. The essay first appeared in 1795; we use the translation of the second and third articles (London, 1796).

The public right ought to be founded upon a federation of free states.

Nations, as states, like individuals, if they live in a state of nature and without laws, by their vicinity alone commit an act of lesion. One may, in order to secure its own safety, require of another to establish within it a constitution which should guarantee to all their rights. This would be a federation of nations, without the people however forming one and the same state, the idea of a state supposing the relation of a sovereign to the people, of a superior to his inferior. Now several nations, united into one state, would no longer form but one; which contradicts the supposition, the question here being of the reciprocal rights of nations, inasmuch as they compose a multitude of different states, which ought not to be incorporated into one and the same state.

But when we see savages in their anarchy, prefer the perpetual combats of licentious liberty to a reasonable liberty, founded upon constitutional order, can we refrain to look down with the most profound contempt on this animal degradation of humanity? Must we not blush at the contempt to which the want of civilization reduces men? And would one not rather be led to think that civilized nations, each of which form a constituted state, would

hasten to extricate themselves from an order of things so ignomini-
ous? But what, on the contrary, do we behold? Every state placing
its majesty (for it is absurd to talk of the majesty of the people)
precisely in this independence of every constraint of any external
legislation whatever.

The sovereign places his glory in the power of disposing at his
pleasure (without much exposing himself) of many millions of men,
ever ready to sacrifice themselves for an object that does not concern them. The only difference between the savages of America
and those of Europe, is, that the former have eaten up many a
hostile tribe, whereas the latter have known how to make a better
use of their enemies; they preserve them to augment the number
of their subjects, that is to say, of instruments destined to more
extensive conquests. When we consider the perverseness of human
nature, which shews itself unveiled and unrestrained in the relations of nations with each other, where it is not checked, as in
a state of civilization, by the coercive power of the law, one may
well be astonished that the word right has not yet been totally
abolished from war-politics as a pedantic word, and that a state
has not yet been found bold enough openly to profess this doctrine.
For hitherto Grotius, Puffendorf, Vattel, and other useless and
impotent defenders of the rights of nations, have been constantly
cited in justification of war; though their code, purely philosophic
or diplomatic, has never had the force of law, and cannot obtain
it; states not being as yet subjected to any coercive power. There
is no instance where their reasonings, supported by such respectable authorities, have induced a state to desist from its pretentions.
However this homage which all states render to the principle of
right, if even consisting only in words, is a proof of a moral disposition, which, though still slumbering, tends nevertheless vigor-
ously to subdue in man that evil principle, of which he cannot
entirely divest himself. For otherwise states would never pronounce the word right, when going to war with each other; it
were then ironically, as a Gallic prince interpreted it. "It is," said
he, "the prerogative nature has given to the stronger, to make
himself obeyed by the weaker."

However, the field of battle is the only tribunal before which
states plead their cause; but victory, by gaining the suit, does

not decide in favour of their cause. Though the treaty of peace puts an end to the present war, it does not abolish a state of war (a state where continually new pretences for war are found); which one cannot affirm to be unjust, since being their own judges, they have no other means of terminating their differences. The law of nations cannot even force them, as the law of nature obliges individuals to get free from this state of war, since having already a legal constitution, as states, they are secure against every foreign compulsion, which might tend to establish among them a more extended constitutional order.

Since, however, from her highest tribunal of moral legislation, reason without exception condemns war as a mean of right, and makes a state of peace an absolute duty; and since this peace cannot be effected or be guaranteed without a compact among nations, they must form an alliance of a peculiar kind, which might be called a pacific alliance different from a treaty of peace inasmuch as it would for ever terminate all wars, whereas the latter only finishes one. This alliance does not tend to any dominion over a state, but solely to the certain maintenance of the liberty of each particular state, partaking of this association, without being therefore obliged to submit, like men in a state of nature, to the legal constraint of public force. It can be proved, that the idea of a federation, which should insensibly extend to all states, and thus lead them to a perpetual peace, may be realized. For if fortune should so direct, that a people as powerful as enlightened, should constitute itself into a republic (a government which in its nature inclines to a perpetual peace) from that time there would be a centre for this federative association; other states might adhere thereto, in order to guarantee their liberty according to the principles of public right; and this alliance might insensibly be extended.

That a people should say, "There shall not be war among us: we will form ourselves into a state; that is to say, we will ourselves establish a legislative, executive, and judiciary power, to decide our differences,"—can be conceived.

But if this state should say, "There shall not be war between us and other states, although we do not acknowledge a supreme power, that guarantees our reciprocal rights;" upon what then can this confidence in one's rights be founded, except it is upon this free federation, this supplement of the social compact, which reason necessarily associates with the idea of public right.

The expression of public right, taken in a sense of right of war, presents properly no idea to the mind; since thereby is understood a power of deciding right, not according to universal laws, which restrain within the same limits all individuals, but according to partial maxims, namely, by force. Except one would wish to insinuate by this expression, that it is right, that men who admit such principles should destroy each other, and thus find perpetual peace only in the vast grave that swallows them and their iniquities.

At the tribunal of reason, there is but one means of extricating states from this turbulent situation, in which they are constantly menaced with war; namely, to renounce, like individuals, the anarchic liberty of savages, in order to submit themselves to coercive laws, and thus form a society of nations (*civitas gentium*) which would insensibly embrace all the nations of the earth. But as the ideas which they have of public right, absolutely prevent the realization of this plan, and make them reject in practice what is true in theory, there can only be substituted, to the positive idea of an universal republic (if all is not to be lost) the negative supplement of a permanent alliance, which prevents war, insensibly spreads, and stops the torrent of those unjust and inhuman passions, which always threaten to break down this fence.

The cosmopolitical right shall be limited to conditions of universal hospitality.

In this article, as well as in the preceding ones, it is a question of right, not of philanthropy. Hospitality there signifies solely the right every stranger has of not being treated as an enemy in the country in which he arrives. One may refuse to receive him, if it can be done without endangering his existence; but dares not act hostily towards him, so long as he does not offend any one. The question is not about the right of being received and admitted into the house of an individual: this benevolent custom demanding particular conventions. One speaks here only of the right all men have, of demanding of others to be admitted into their society; a right founded upon that of the common possession of the surface of the earth, whose spherical form obliges them to suffer others to subsist contiguous to them, because they cannot disperse themselves to an indefinite distance, and because originally one has not a greater right to a country than another. The sea and uninhabitable desarts divide the surface of the globe; but the ship and the camel, that vessel of the desart, re-establish the communication and facilitate the right which the human species all possess, of profiting in common by its surface. The inhospitality of the inhabitants of the coasts (for instance of the coast of Barbary) their custom of taking the vessels in the neighbouring seas, or that of reducing to slavery the unhappy wretches shipwrecked on their shores; the barbarous practice which in their sandy deserts the Bedouin Arabs exercise of pillaging all those who approach their wandering tribes; all these customs then are contrary to the right of nature, which, nevertheless, in ordaining hospitality, was contented with fixing the conditions on which one may endeavour to form connections with the inhabitants of a country. In this manner distant regions may contract amicable relations with each other, sanctioned in the end by public laws, and thus insensibly mankind may approach towards a cosmopolitical constitution.

At how great a distance from this perfection are the civilized nations, and especially the commercial nations of Europe? At what an excess of injustice do we not behold them arrived, when they discover strange countries and nations? (which with them is the same thing as to conquer). America, the countries inhabited by the negroes, the Spice Islands, the Cape, &c. were to them countries without proprietors, for the inhabitants they counted as nothing. Under pretext of establishing factories in Hindostan, they carried thither foreign troops, and by their means oppressed the natives, excited wars among the different states of that vast country; spread famine, rebellion, perfidy, and the whole deluge of evils that afflict mankind, among them.

The Chinese and Japanese, whom experience has taught to know the Europeans, wisely refuse their entry into the country, though the former permit their approach, which the latter grant to one European nation only, the Dutch; still, however, excluding them like captives from every communication with the inhabitants.

The worst, or to speak with the moralist, the best of the matter is, that all these outrages are to no purpose; that all the commercial companies, guilty of them, touch upon the instant of their ruin; that the sugar islands, that den of slavery the most refined and cruel, produce no real revenue, and are profitable only indirectly, serving views not very laudable, namely, to form sailors for the navies, consequently to carry on war in Europe; which service they render to powers who boast the most of piety, and who, whilst they drink iniquity like water, pretend to equal the elect in point of orthodoxy.

The connections, more or less near, which have taken place among the nations of the earth, having been carried to that point, that a violation of rights, committed in one place, is felt throughout the whole, the idea of a cosmopolitical right can no longer pass for a fantastic exaggeration of right; but is the last step of perfection necessary to the tacit code of civil and public right; these systems at length conducting towards a public right of men in general, and towards a perpetual peace, but to which one cannot hope continually to advance, except by means of the conditions here indicated.

4. Condorcet: Future Progress of Mankind

The excerpt is from the "Tenth Epoch" of the *Outlines of an Historical View of the Progress of the Human Mind* by Marie Jean Antoine Nicolas Caritat, Marquis de Condorcet. Nine preceding chapters had already depicted the history of mankind from the earliest stages of civilization through the present. Condorcet, a Secretary of the Academy of Sciences before the Revolution, a mathematician, a Girondist politician, and a prolific pamphleteer on behalf of his party, wrote this last testament to humanity while he was hiding from Robespierre's police in a Paris garret. We use the translation printed at Philadelphia in 1796. There had been a London edition of the work the previous year, immediately upon its appearance in France in 1795.

If man can predict, almost with certainty, those appearances of which he understands the laws; if, even when the laws are unknown to him, experience or the past enables him to foresee, with considerable probability, future appearances; why should we suppose it a chimerical undertaking to delineate, with some degree of truth, the picture of the future destiny of mankind from the results of its history? The only foundation of faith in the natural sciences is the principle, that the general laws, known or unknown, which regulate the phenomena of the universe, are regular and constant; and why should this principle, applicable to the other operations of nature, be less true when applied to the development of the intellectual and moral faculties of man? In short, as opinions formed from experience, relative to the same class of objects, are the only rule by which men of soundest understanding are governed in their conduct, why should the philosopher be proscribed from supporting his conjectures upon a similar basis, provided he attribute to them no greater certainty than the number, the consistency, and the accuracy of actual observations shall authorise?

Our hopes, as to the future condition of the human species, may be reduced to three points: the destruction of inequality between different nations; the progress of equality in one and the same nation; and lastly, the real improvement of man.

Will not every nation one day arrive at the state of civilization attained by those people who are most enlightened, most free, most exempt from prejudices, as the French, for instance, and the Anglo-Americans? Will not slavery of countries subjected to kings, the barbarity of African tribes, and the ignorance of savages gradually vanish? Is there upon the face of the globe a single spot the inhabitants of which are condemned by nature never to enjoy liberty, never to exercise their reason?

Does the difference of knowledge, of means, and of wealth, observable hitherto in all civilized nations, between the classes into which the people constituting those nations are divided; does that inequality which the earliest progress of society has augmented, or, to speak more properly, produced, belong to civilization itself, or to the imperfections of the social order? Must it not continually weaken, in order to give place to that actual equality, the chief end of the social art, which diminishing even the effects of the natural difference of the faculties, leaves no other inequality subsisting but what is useful to the interest of all, because it will favour civilization, instruction, and industry, without drawing after it either dependence, humiliation or poverty? In a word, will not men be continually verging towards that state, in which all will possess the requisite knowledge for conducting themselves in the common affairs of life by their own reason, and of maintaining that reason uncontaminated by prejudices; in which they will understand their rights, and exercise them according to their opinion and their conscience; in which all will be able, by the developement of their faculties, to procure the certain means of providing for their wants; lastly, in which folly and wretchedness will be accidents, happening only now and then, and not the habitual lot of a considerable portion of society?

In fine, may it not be expected that the human race will be meliorated by new discoveries in the sciences and the arts, and, as an unavoidable consequence, in the means of individual and general prosperity; by farther progress in the principles of conduct, and in moral practice; and lastly, by the real improvement of our faculties, moral, intellectual and physical, which may be the result either of the improvement of the instruments which increase the power and direct the exercise of those faculties, or of the improvement of our natural organization itself?

In examining the three questions we have enumerated, we shall find the strongest reasons to believe, from past experience, from observation of the progress which the sciences and civilization have hitherto made, and from the analysis of the march of the human understanding, and the development of its faculties, that nature has fixed no limits to our hopes.

If we take a survey of the existing state of the globe, we shall perceive, in the first place, that in Europe the principles of the French constitution are those of every enlightened mind. We shall perceive that they are too widely disseminated, and too openly professed, for the efforts of tyrants and priests to prevent them from penetrating by degrees into the miserable cottages of their slaves, where they will soon revive those embers of good sense, and rouse that silent indignation which the habit of suffering and terror have failed totally to extinguish in the minds of the oppressed.

If we next look at the different nations, we shall observe in each, particular obstacles opposing, or certain dispositions favouring this revolution. We shall distinguish some in which it will be effected, perhaps slowly, by the wisdom of the respective governments; and others in which, rendered violent by resistance, the governments themselves will necessarily be involved in its terrible and rapid motions.

Can it be supposed that either the wisdom or the senseless feuds of European nations, co-operating with the slow but certain effects of the progress of their colonies, will not shortly produce the independence of the entire new world; and that then, European population, lending its aid, will fail to civilize or cause to disappear, even without conquest, those savage nations still occupying there immense tracts of country?

Run through the history of our projects and establishments in Africa or in Asia, and you will see our monopolies, our treachery, our sanguinary contempt for men of a different complexion or different creed, and the proselyting fury or the intrigues of our priests, destroying that sentiment of respect and benevolence which the superiority of our information and the advantages of our commerce had at first obtained.

But the period is doubtless approaching, when, no longer exhibiting to the view of these people corruptors only or tyrants, we shall become to them instruments of benefit, and the generous champions of their redemption from bondage.

The progress of the sciences secures the progress of the art of instruction, which again accelerates in its turn that of the sciences; and this reciprocal influence, the action of which is incessantly increased, must be ranked in the number of the most prolific and powerful causes of the improvement of the human race. At present, a young man, upon finishing his studies and quitting our schools, may know more of the principles of mathematics than Newton acquired by profound study, or discovered by the force of his genius, and may exercise the instrument of calculation with a readiness which at that period was unknown. The same observation, with certain restrictions, may be applied to all the sciences. In proportion as each shall advance, the means of compressing, within a smaller circle, the proofs of a greater number of truths, and of facilitating their comprehension, will equally advance. Thus, notwithstanding future degrees of progress, not only will men of equal genius find themselves, at the same period of life, upon a level with the actual state of science, but, respecting every generation, what may be acquired in a given space of time, by the same strength of intellect and the same degree of attention, will necessarily increase, and the elementary part of each science, that part which every man may attain, becoming more and more extended, will include, in a manner more complete, the knowledge necessary for the direction of every man in the common occurrences of life, and for the free and independent exercise of his reason.

In the political sciences there is a description of truths, which particularly in free countries (that is, in all countries in certain generations), can only be useful when generally known and avowed. Thus, the influence of these sciences upon the freedom and prosperity of nations, must, in some sort, be measured by the number of those truths that, in consequence of elementary instruction, shall pervade the general mind; and thus, as the growing progress of this elementary instruction is connected with the necessary progress of the sciences, we may expect a melioration in the doctrines of the human race which may be regarded as indefinite, since it can have no other limits than those of the two species of progress on which it depends.

We have still two other means of general application to consider, and which must influence at once both the improvement of the art of instruction and that of the sciences. One is a more extensive and more perfect adoption of what may be called technical methods; the other, the institution of an universal language.

It might be shown that the formation of such a language, if confined to the expressing of simple and precise propositions, like those which form the system of a science, or the practice of an art, would be the reverse of chimerical; that its execution, even at present, would be extremely practicable as to a great number of objects; and that the chief obstacle that would stand in the way of extending it to others, would be the humiliating necessity of acknowledging how few precise ideas, and accurately defined notions, understood exactly in the same sense by every mind, we really possess.

It might be shown that this language, improving every day, acquiring incessantly greater extent, would be the means of giving to every object that comes within the reach of human intelligence, a rigour, and precision, that would facilitate the knowledge of truth, and render error almost impossible. Then would the march of every science be as infallible as that of the mathematics, and the propositions of every system acquire, as far as nature will admit, geometrical demonstration and certainty.

All the causes which contribute to the improvement of the human species, all the means we have enumerated that insure its progress, must, from their very nature, exercise an influence always active, and acquire an extent for ever increasing. The proofs of this have been exhibited, and from their development in the work itself they will derive additional force: accordingly we may already conclude, that the perfectibility of man is indefinite. Meanwhile we have hitherto considered him as possessing only the same natural faculties, as endowed with the same organization. How much greater would be the certainty, how much wider the compass of our hopes, could we prove that these natural faculties themselves, that this very organization, are also susceptible of melioration? And this is the last question we shall examine.

The organic perfectibility or deterioration of the classes of the vegetable, or species of the animal kingdom, may be regarded as one of the general laws of nature.

This law extends itself to the human race; and it cannot be doubted that the progress of the sanative art, that the use of more wholesome food and more comfortable habitations, that a mode of life which shall develope the physical powers by exercise, without at the same time impairing them by excess; in fine, that the destruction of the two most active causes of deterioration, penury and wretchedness on the one hand, and enormous wealth on the other, must necessarily tend to prolong the common duration of man's existence, and secure him a more constant health and a more robust constitution. It is manifest that the improvement of the practice of medicine, become more efficacious in consequence of the progress of reason and the social order, must in the end put a period to transmissible or contagious disorders, as well to those general maladies resulting from climate, aliments, and the nature of certain occupations. Nor would it be difficult to prove that this hope might be extended to almost every other malady, of which it is probable we shall hereafter discover the most remote causes. Would it even be absurd to suppose this quality of melioration in the human species as susceptible of an indefinite advancement; to suppose that a period must one day arrive when death will be nothing more than the effect either of extraordinary accidents, or of the slow and gradual decay of the vital powers; and that the duration of the middle space, of the interval between the birth of man and this decay, will itself have no assignable limit? Certainly man will not become immortal; but may not the distance between the moment in which he draws his first breath, and the common term when, in the course of nature, without malady or accident, he finds it impossible any longer to exist, be necessarily protracted? As we are now speaking of a progress that is capable of being represented with precision, by numerical quantities or by lines, we shall embrace the opportunity of explaining the two meanings that may be affixed to the word *indefinite*.

In reality, this middle term of life, which in proportion as men advance upon the ocean of futurity, we have supposed incessantly to increase, may receive additions either in conformity to a law by which, though approaching continually an illimitable extent, it could never possibly arrive at it; or a law by which, in the immensity of ages, it may acquire a greater extent than any determinate quantity whatever that may be assigned as its limit. In the latter case, this duration of life is indefinite in the strictest sense of the word, since there exist no bounds on this side of which it must necessarily stop. And in the former, it is equally indefinite to us; if we cannot fix the term, it may for ever approach, but can never surpass; particularly if, knowing only that it can never stop, we are ignorant in which of the two senses the term indefinite is applicable to it: and this is precisely the state of the knowledge we have as yet acquired relative to the perfectibility of the species.

Thus, in the instance we are considering, we are bound to believe that the mean duration of human life will for ever increase, unless its increase be prevented by the physical revolutions of the system; but we cannot tell what is the bound which the duration of human life can never exceed; we cannot even tell, whether there be any circumstance in the laws of nature which has determined and laid down its limit.

But may not our physical faculties, the force, the sagacity, the acuteness of the senses, be numbered among the qualities, the individual improvement of which it will be practicable to transmit? An attention to the different breeds of domestic animals must lead us to adopt the affirmative of this question, and a direct observation of the human species itself will be found to strengthen the opinion.

Lastly, may we not include in the same circle the intellectual and moral faculties? May not our parents, who transmit to us the advantages or defects of their conformation, and from whom we receive our features and shape, as well as our propensities to certain physical affections, transmit to us also that part of organization upon which intellect, strength of understanding, energy of soul or moral sensibility depend? Is it not probable that education, by improving these qualities, will at the same time have an influence upon, will modify and improve this organization itself? Analogy, an investigation of the human faculties, and even some facts, appear to authorise these conjectures, and thereby to enlarge the boundary of our hopes.

Such are the questions with which we shall terminate the last division of our work. And how admirably calculated is this view of the human race, emancipated from its chains, released alike from the dominion of chance, as well as from that of the enemies of its progress, and advancing with a firm and inevitate step in the paths of truth, to console the philosopher lamenting the errors, the flagrant acts of injustice, the crimes with which the earth is still polluted? It is the contemplation of this prospect that rewards him for all his efforts to assist the progress of reason and the establishment of liberty. He dares to regard these efforts as a part of the eternal chain of the destiny of mankind; and in this persuasion he finds the true delight of virtue, the pleasure of having performed a durable service, which no vicissitude will ever destroy in a fatal operation calculated to restore the reign of prejudice and slavery. This sentiment is the asylum into which he retires, and to which the memory of his persecutors cannot follow him; he unites himself in imagination with man restored to his rights, delivered from oppression, and proceeding with rapid strides in the path of happiness; he forgets his own misfortunes while his thoughts are thus employed; he lives no longer to adversity, calumny and malice, but becomes the associate of these wiser and more fortunate beings whose enviable condition he so earnestly contributed to produce.